DÜRER'S FAME

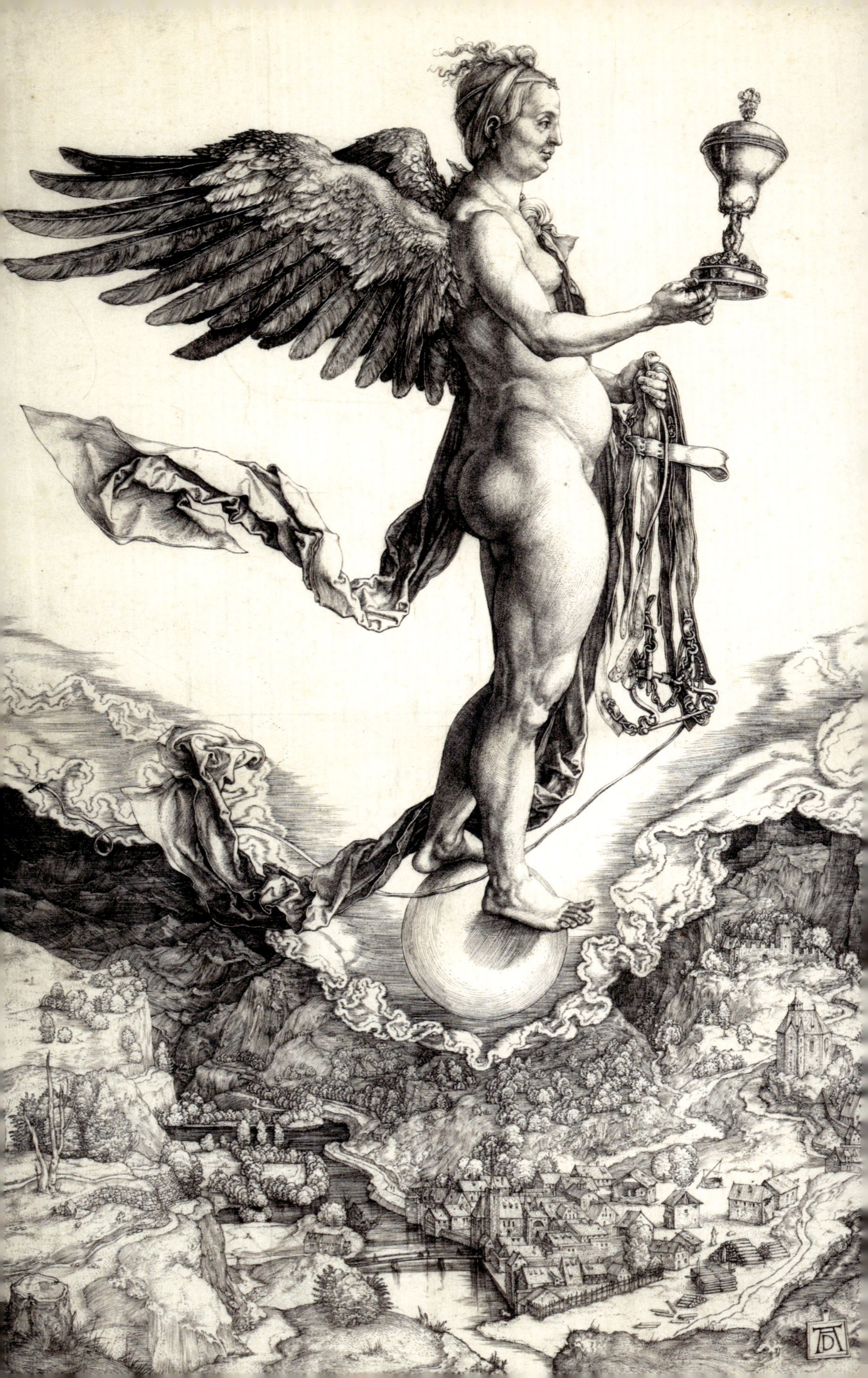

Christian Tico Seifert

DÜRER'S FAME

National Galleries of Scotland
Edinburgh 2011

Published by the Trustees of the National Galleries of Scotland to accompany the exhibition *Dürer's Fame* held at the National Gallery Complex, Edinburgh from 9 June to 11 October 2011.

ISBN 978 1 906270 41 4

Designed and typeset in Adobe Jenson by Dalrymple
Printed on Hello Matt 170gsm by OZGraf SA, Poland

Cover: details from Albrecht Dürer, *Saint Jerome in his Study* 1514, National Gallery of Scotland, Edinburgh (fig.1)

Frontispiece: Albrecht Dürer, *Nemesis (The Large Fortune)*, *c.*1501, National Gallery of Scotland, Edinburgh

The proceeds from the sale of this book go towards supporting the National Galleries of Scotland. For a complete list of current publications, please write to NGS Publishing, Scottish National Gallery of Modern Art, Edinburgh EH4 3DR, or visit our website: www.nationalgalleries.org

National Galleries of Scotland is a charity registered in Scotland (no.SC003728)

NATIONAL
GALLERIES
SCOTLAND

CONTENTS

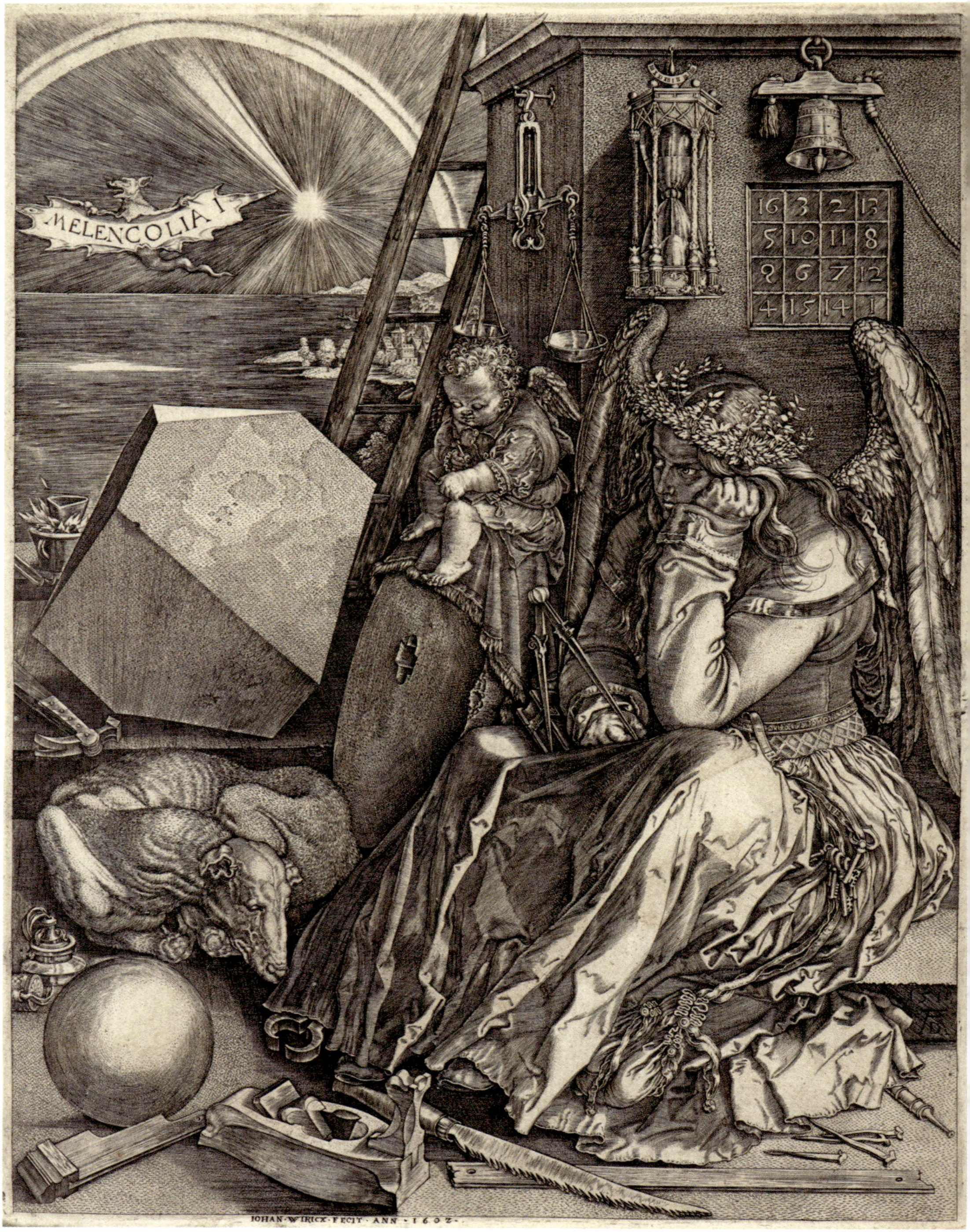

Johannes Wierix (after Albrecht Dürer), *Melencolia I*
(Melancholy), 1602, National Gallery of Scotland, Edinburgh

FOREWORD

THE NATIONAL GALLERY OF SCOTLAND HAS A SMALL COLLECTION of prints by Albrecht Dürer, the most important artist of the Northern Renaissance. Among these are a number of superb impressions, most of which were acquired by the renowned former Keeper of Prints and Drawings, Keith Andrews (1920–1989). Few of the Gallery's Dürer prints have been exhibited since the 500th anniversary of the artist's birth in 1971. *Dürer's Fame* puts a selection of works by Dürer in context and shows, complemented with objects from the Scottish National Portrait Gallery, their impact and creative reception over the centuries, including works by Scottish artists such as John Runciman and William Bell Scott, whose response to Dürer's art is explored in this innovative exhibition.

Dürer's Fame has been devised and organised by our colleague, Dr Tico Seifert, Senior Curator at the National Gallery of Scotland. Research for this book was kindly supported by the German Consulate General Edinburgh. Publication was made possible through the generous support of Martin Adam and William Zachs.

JOHN LEIGHTON
Director-General, National Galleries of Scotland

MICHAEL CLARKE
Director, National Gallery of Scotland

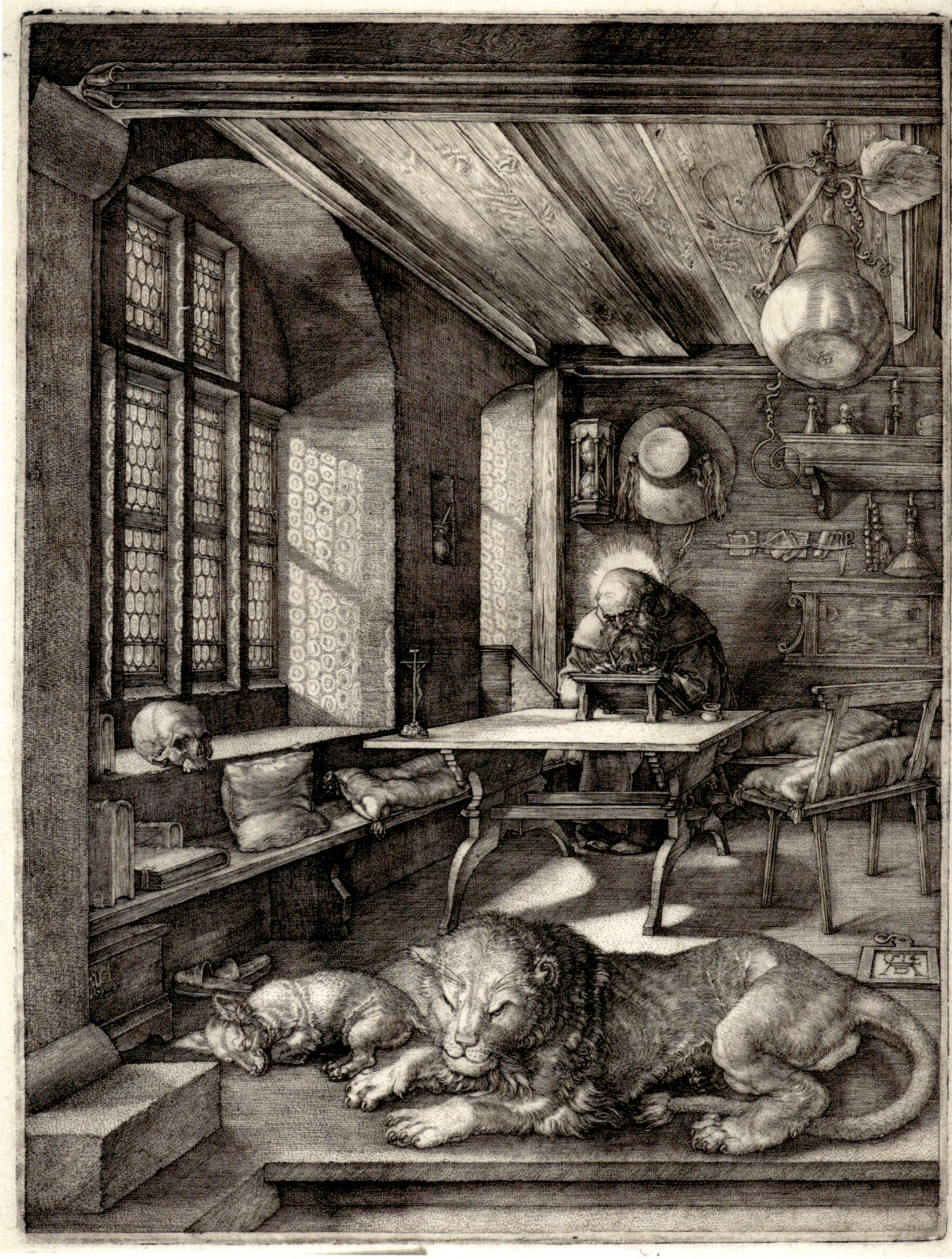

[Fig.1] Albrecht Dürer, *Saint Jerome in his Study*, 1514, National Gallery of Scotland, Edinburgh

DÜRER'S FAME

ALBRECHT DÜRER IS ONE OF THE MOST FAMOUS ARTISTS of all times. He excelled as a painter, draughtsman and printmaker and received major commissions from Emperor Maximilian I and princely patrons. Dürer was a learned artist, had friends among the German humanist circles, and his books on perspective and human proportion are the first art theoretical treatises in German. He visited Italy twice and travelled to the Netherlands. His contemporary fame and subsequent reputation across Europe rests on his technical brilliance, his highly individual approach to subject matter and his extraordinary interest in nature and the human figure. Dürer's nature studies and landscape watercolours are among the most beautiful ever made. He explored mythological, biblical and apocryphal scenes, allegories and portraits, single devotional figures and everyday scenes. Above all, his prints spread his fame across Europe during his lifetime, and continue to do so today.

Given the modest size of the Dürer collection in the National Galleries of Scotland, it would be over-ambitious to try to give a comprehensive account of the artist's work and legacy, as the British Museum did very successfully in 2002. This book, therefore, examines different aspects of the artist's fame, presenting a selection of his prints, together with contemporary and later copies and imitations, as well as portraits and works that reflect not only Dürer's art but also the collecting of his art. Telling the story of his fame through these objects will hopefully add small pieces to the enormous mosaic of Dürer's art and reputation.

THE PRINTMAKER'S FAME

A few weeks before Albrecht Dürer died on 6 April 1528 at the age of fifty-six, the great humanist Erasmus of Rotterdam compared him to Apelles, the most famous painter of antiquity. This was a commonplace in eulogies on painters. Erasmus, however, did not refer to Dürer as a painter but as a printmaker: 'Dürer ... what does he not express in monochromes, that is, by black lines? Shade, light, radiance, eminences, depressions ... Nay, he even depicts what cannot be depicted: fire, rays of light, thunderstorms, sheet lightning ... These things he places before our eyes by most felicitous lines, black ones that is ... And is it not more wonderful to accomplish without the blandishment of colours what Apelles accomplished [only] with their aid?'[1] Dürer's fame for his contemporaries and for centuries to come was mainly based on the astonishing quality and revolutionary technique of his prints (fig.1).

Young Dürer became familiar with the skills of printmaking early on. Born in Nuremberg, the son of a goldsmith, he trained there first with his father and then with their neighbour Michael Wolgemut. The latter was the most important painter in the city, whose workshop also produced huge numbers of woodcut illustrations for the flourishing Nuremberg publishers. After four years of *Wanderjahre*, the traditional travel following an apprenticeship, Dürer returned to his native city only briefly in 1494. He married Agnes Frey and soon set out for Italy, and on his return he set up his own workshop in Nuremberg in 1495.[2]

Dürer was a prolific, versatile and highly innovative printmaker. Moreover, he was the first artist who excelled in all the major printmaking techniques. As an apprentice he had possibly contributed to the Wolgemut print production and designed woodcuts for book illustrations during his *Wanderjahre*. Around 1495 Dürer also started engraving and he later experimented with etching on iron plates (fig.2) and drypoint. He developed engraving and woodcutting to a quality of technique, form and expression unrivalled in his age, and it has been noted that 'Dürer effectively made woodcut an extension of engraving' – transferring the intaglio line of the copperplate into a line cut in relief into the woodblock.[3] Consequently, Dürer was the first artist consistently signing not only his engravings but also his woodcuts, raising what was considered a craft to an art (fig.3). The

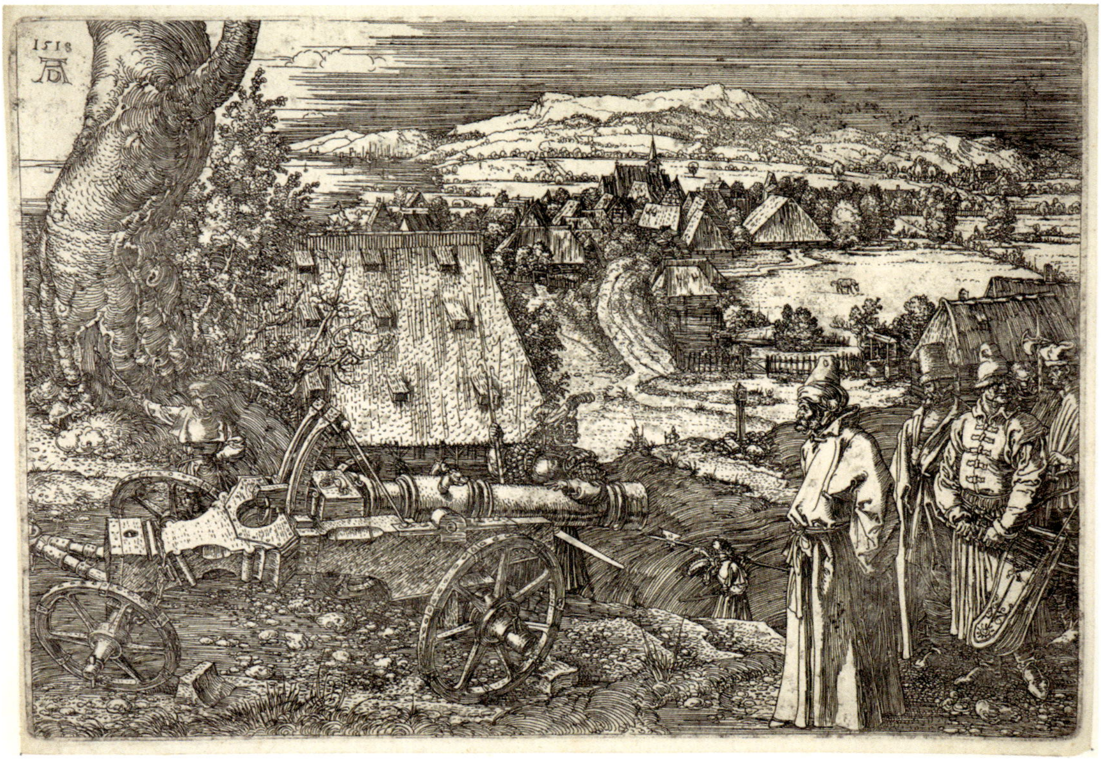

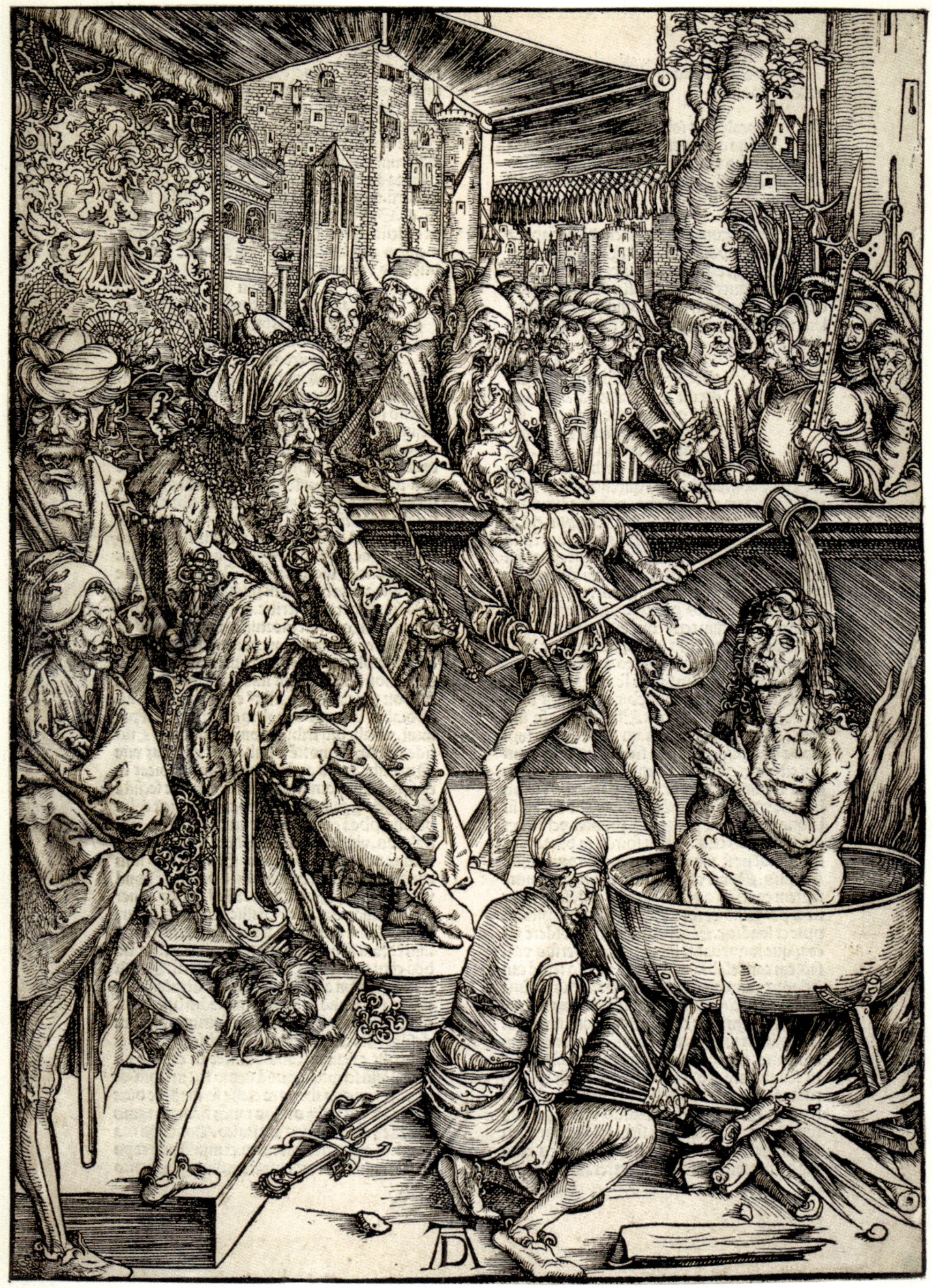

left [Fig.2] Albrecht Dürer, *Landscape with the Cannon*, 1518, National Gallery of Scotland, Edinburgh

above [Fig.3] Albrecht Dürer, *The Martyrdom of Saint John*, c.1496–7, from *The Apocalypse*, National Gallery of Scotland, Edinburgh

question whether he himself cut his designs into the blocks, at least early in his career, remains much debated.[4] However, given the traditional distinction between the designer, the *Reisser*, who transfers the drawing onto the woodblock, and the woodcutter, the number of highly skilled woodcutters in Nuremberg, and the time-consuming business of woodcutting, it seems likely that Dürer rarely if ever exchanged the burin for the knife.

As Erasmus pointed out, Dürer expressed his art, as far as printmaking is concerned, exclusively in black and white. He never coloured any of his prints, a fashion still very popular in the early sixteenth century. Nor did he produce any chiaroscuro woodcuts, which combine mostly black line blocks with coloured tone blocks, a technique in which his contemporaries Lucas Cranach and Hans Burgkmair excelled. Dürer instead challenged the boundaries of monochrome printmaking techniques, creating form and tone, light and shade, atmosphere and expression with black lines on white paper exclusively.

Despite all these achievements, Dürer regarded himself a painter rather than a printmaker. In 1498 he signed the colophon of the first edition of *The Apocalypse* 'Albrecht Dürer maler (painter)'. The status and reputation of the painter greatly exceeded that of the printmaker, whose art (in contrast to craft) had not yet been established in its own right. Moreover, paintings were elaborate, unique art works, expensive and long-lasting, while prints were serial products, of comparably little material value and easily worn.

What then sparked and nurtured Dürer's interest in printmaking? Certainly, the artistic challenge was an important motivation and Dürer (and at least some of his audience) realised that his prints were artworks in their own right, containing the artist's idea and design to the same degree as any painting. But Dürer was also acutely aware of the other advantages of prints. Once the plate or block was completed, a large number of impressions could be produced. These multiple artworks were instantly available to the artist and his clients. Prints could easily be sold and distributed over long distances, delivering financial benefit and spreading his art and fame much more quickly and effectively than paintings could ever have done.

Towards the end of his life Dürer was probably the most famous artist north of the Alps. That he thoroughly enjoyed his fame is obvious from the journal he kept while travelling in the Netherlands with his wife from 1520 to 1521. He described, with satisfaction, the dinner the Antwerp painters' guild gave in his honour: 'And when I was being conducted to the table all the people stood up on each side as if they were leading a great lord. There were amongst them, also many persons of distinction, who all bowed low in the most humble manner.'[5] Visiting Ghent, Dürer was, again, well received by the local authorities who accompanied him to Jan van Eyck's renowned altarpiece. More than three hundred years later, in about 1840, the Ghent painters Pieter Frans de Noter and Felix de Vigne depicted this scene (fig.4).[6] Dürer's visit to Ghent had become famous itself and was celebrated by de Noter and de Vigne to highlight their city's importance.

FAME MULTIPLIED: COPIES

Dürer's prints were copied from very early on, the copyists motivated mostly by commercial success.[7] Dürer kept his plates and woodblocks under his own control in order to supervise the quality and limit the number of impressions. Copyists, however, circumvented the artist's monopoly and produced their own prints for an ever-growing market. During Dürer's lifetime more than 250 different copies after his prints were produced north of the Alps alone.[8] One of the early northern copyists was Hieronymus Greff. In 1502, four years after Dürer's first edition of *The Apocalypse*, Greff issued a copy of the work in Strasbourg (fig.5).[9] He faithfully reproduced Dürer's designs, by using the same woodcut technique, keeping the exact dimensions and orientation, but replacing Dürer's monogram with his own. Only knowledgeable clients would realise that Greff's prints were copies after *The Apocalypse* by Dürer.

The most famous of the Italian copyists, the Bolognese printmaker Marcantonio Raimondi did quite the opposite, at least initially. Not only did he retain Dürer's monogram but also he did not reveal his own identity as the actual engraver. The Florentine artist and biographer Giorgio Vasari, in the second edition of his *Lives of the Most Eminent Painters,*

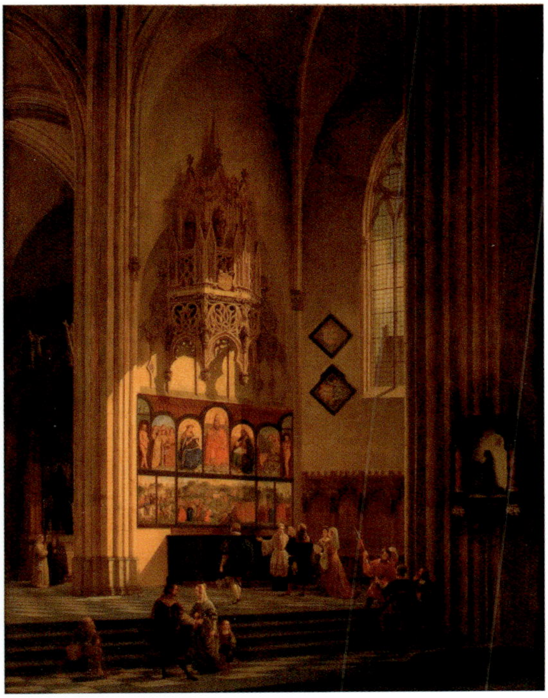

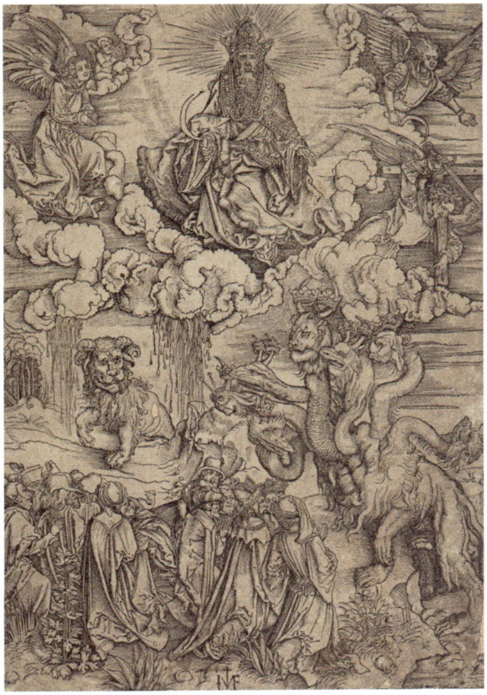

[Fig.4] Pieter Frans de Noter and Felix de Vigne, *Albrecht Dürer Viewing Jan van Eyck's 'Ghent Altarpiece'*, c.1840, Rijksmuseum Twenthe, Enschede

[Fig.5] Hieronymus Greff (after Albrecht Dürer), *The Beast with Two Horns Like a Lamb*, 1502, from *The Apocalypse*, National Gallery of Scotland, Edinburgh

Sculptors and Architects (1568) gave a lively account of the events. Raimondi had seen Dürer's prints in Venice and astonished by Dürer's style and technique, Raimondi started 'copying' these prints, 'studying the character of the lines and the prints as a whole'. Vasari also relates that Dürer's prints were highly sought after and that Raimondi transferred Dürer's woodcuts into engravings, including the latter's monogram, so that they were taken for the German master's works. According to Vasari, Dürer was infuriated when he received the copies, set out for Venice and complained about Raimondi to the senate there. However, all that Dürer was able to achieve was that Raimondi was no longer allowed to use his name or monogram on his prints.[10] Scholars have tried to determine the truth of Vasari's anecdote. Raimondi did indeed copy seventeen sheets from *The Life of the Virgin* and Dürer did travel to Italy from 1505 to 1507. However, it is unlikely that Raimondi's copies motivated Dürer's second trip to Italy. The well-preserved Venetian archives contain no documents on this case, nor did Dürer mention it in the letters extant from his second Italian visit. Adding to the confusion, Vasari mistakenly writes of Raimondi copying Dürer's *The Small Passion* which wasn't published until 1511. Vasari, moreover, contradicts himself within two pages. Just before relating the story of Dürer's fury, he states that the German artist on finishing designs (again Vasari mistakenly refers to *The Small Passion*) and having them engraved 'had agreed with Raimondi to publish them jointly'.[11] A literal reading of this passage would make Raimondi and Dürer partners, with the latter authorising supervised copies to control their quality.[12] Raimondi's copy of *The Glorification of the Virgin* (fig.6) from Dürer's *The Life of the Virgin* indeed shows Dürer's monogram and that of Raimondi as well as the device of the publishers Niccolò and Domenico del Gesù. This print does not form part of the sequence of the story and was numbered '17', probably by Raimondi, which makes it the last within the series. As such the inscriptions could be seen as a colophon for the whole series that identified the copyist as well as the 'inventor' Dürer. This interpretation, however, apart from not being confirmed by any documents, poses new questions. Firstly, the assumption would have to be made that at this point Dürer regarded the set of seventeen prints as complete and wished to publish it as such, but he added another three around 1510. Secondly, it is uncertain whether *The Glorification of the Virgin* bore all three marks initially or, as has been proposed, whether Raimondi's and the publisher's devices were added in a second state.[13] Also, Raimondi, after settling in Rome in 1510, continued to produce copies after Dürer prints, most notably the thirty-seven engravings he made around 1515 after *The Small Passion*. Raimondi omitted Dürer's monogram from these and instead only used the empty tablet that had become his signature.[14] Had the partnership broken up? Is Vasari's anecdote about the artists' quarrels, albeit in disguise, referring to this?

Dürer in any case included a fierce warning to 'envious thieves of the work and invention' on the colophon page of the 1511 editions of *The Life of the Virgin*, *The Small Passion*, *The Large Passion*, and *The Apocalypse*.

A Nuremberg council resolution of 1512 shows that Dürer's concerns were justified. The council ruled that a foreigner who had sold prints in front of the town hall, a number of which were fraudulently copied and bore Dürer's monogram, was required to remove the said monograms and sell none of them in the city. Interestingly, in this case as in Vasari's anecdote, the crime was not copying itself but advertising it as an original by means of a false monogram. The Nuremberg council (similar to the Venetian senate, if Vasari was correct) protected Dürer's trademark but not his images.[15] Whatever the legal status of Raimondi's copies may have been, they contributed immensely to the spread of Dürer's art and fame in Italy and beyond.

On his second visit to Venice Dürer became friends with Giovanni

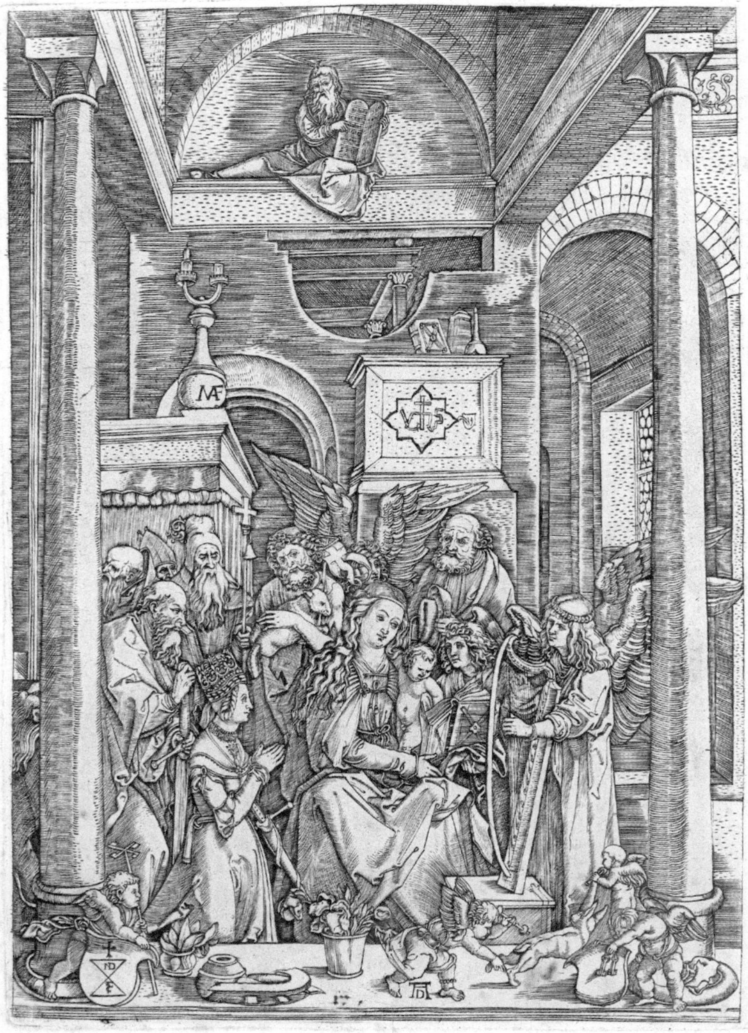

[Fig.6] Marcantonio Raimondi (after Albrecht Dürer),
The Glorification of the Virgin, c.1506, National Gallery of Scotland, Edinburgh

Bellini, the leading painter of the city, then in his mid-seventies.[16] A unique testimony to his reputation among Italian artists is provided by a Raphael drawing that once belonged to Dürer (fig.7).[17] The inscription, which Dürer himself added, states that Raphael had sent him this drawing, most likely in 1515. It is not known when, where, and how the exchange between the two artists first started, but Vasari reports that Dürer had sent Raphael a self-portrait in watercolour on fine canvas, now lost.[18] Apart from this, Raphael's knowledge of Dürer's art would certainly have relied on prints more than anything else. If Dürer and Raimondi had met in Venice, it would be tempting to think that the latter, who worked with Raphael from around 1511 onwards, would have initiated their contact.

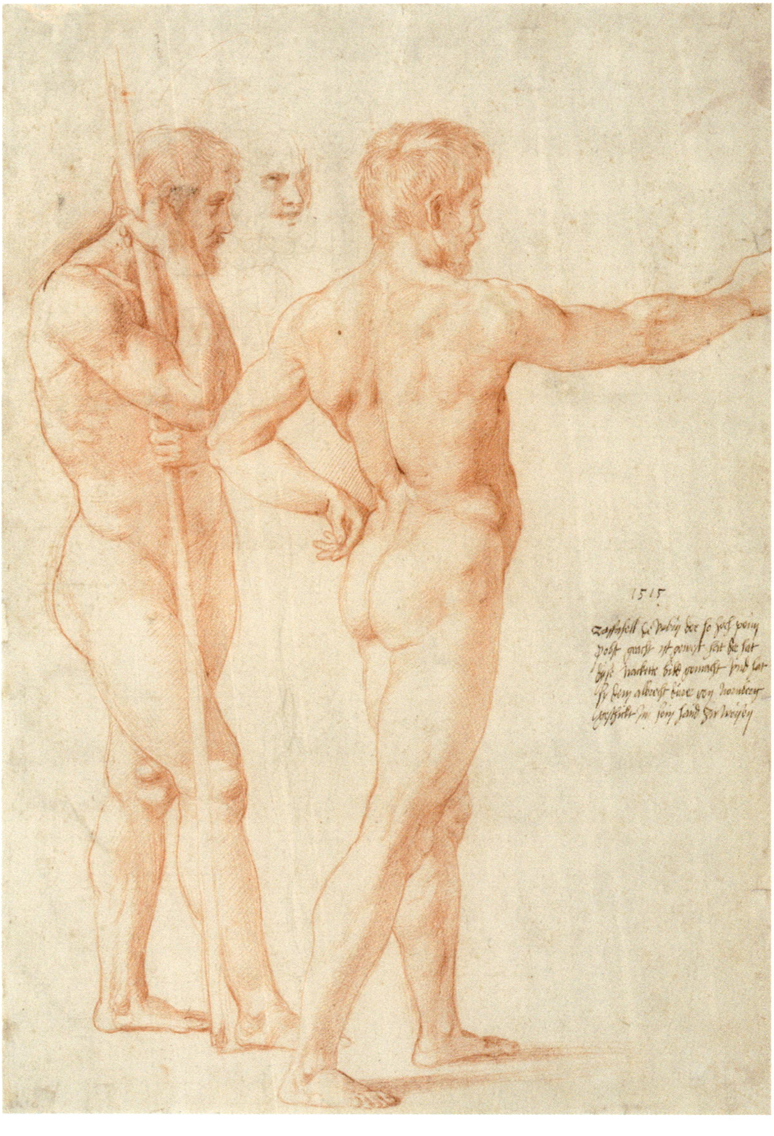

[Fig.7] Raphael, *Studies of Nudes*, 1515, Albertina, Vienna

FAME ADAPTED: INTERPRETATIONS

The example of Dürer's *The Circumcision* from the *The Life of the Virgin* series of woodcuts demonstrates the huge impact of his prints. Dürer's woodcut design of around 1504 (fig.8) was copied in an engraving by Raimondi only two years later (fig.9). The same Dürer print was also the basis for a print of much lesser quality (fig.10) made by an unknown artist and dated (or numbered) '[15]41', though the watermark is similar to ones used in papers from Arnhem from 1604 to 1614. This print is interesting in the way it differs from the iconography of Dürer's woodcut. The engraver of this hitherto unpublished print has omitted any reference to Dürer and replaced the high priest with a bishop wearing a mitre who daringly turns his head towards us while handling the knife; he has also given the figures of Mary and Christ halos. Although Dürer's model is easily recognisable, the printmaker interpreted it differently and adapted the design according to his own needs. As the changes emphasise Mary and the bishop, they possibly indicate a Catholic meaning that would fit into a Counter-Reformation context.

Dürer's *The Circumcision* also inspired Hendrick Goltzius, the preeminent Haarlem-based Dutch printmaker in the late sixteenth century. Around 1600 Goltzius's fame rivalled that of Dürer and in his version of *The Circumcision*, dated 1594 (fig.11), he deliberately challenged the German master. Karel van Mander, the artist and biographer and a close friend of Goltzius, gives an anecdotal account of the artist's ambitions and virtuosity in his *Schilder-boek* of 1604, a treatise and collection of artists' biographies. Goltzius transferred the scene to the Brewers' Chapel of Saint Bavo in Haarlem, included his self-portrait and monogram and executed the print in the style of Dürer. Afterwards, Goltzius burned out his mark and image, repaired and artificially aged the impressions and thus deceived colleagues and collectors all over Europe, as these prints were widely accepted as an unknown engraving by the Nuremberg master. Only after producing a fresh impression of his print did Goltzius's authorship become clear and he was praised for his mastery – and blamed for his joke.[19] Van Mander's story is corroborated by a letter from the Leyden anatomist and botanist Pieter Pauw. In 1594, immediately after the publication of the print, Pauw referred to *The Circumcision* as the 'Albert Dürer-ish piece by Goltzius'.[20]

But the reception of Dürer's *The Circumcision* was neither restricted to Northern Europe nor to the sixteenth century, as a rather large drawing of a man holding a candlestick demonstrates (fig.12). The artist shows the figure isolated against a background of partly ruined architectural features. This sheet has hitherto been classified as an anonymous German copy after Dürer. Recently, however, the drawing has been identified as Neapolitan, from around 1620 to 1630, with a tentative attribution to Jusepe de Ribera.[21] Given the sharp profile and the prominent nose and chin, it seems likely that Ribera worked directly from Dürer's woodcut, as all other copies tend to smooth these features. That Ribera emphasised

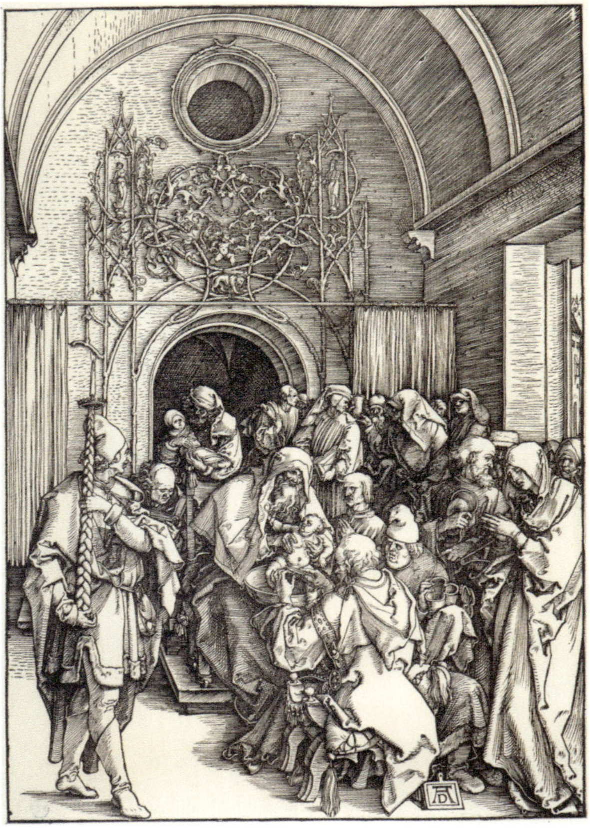

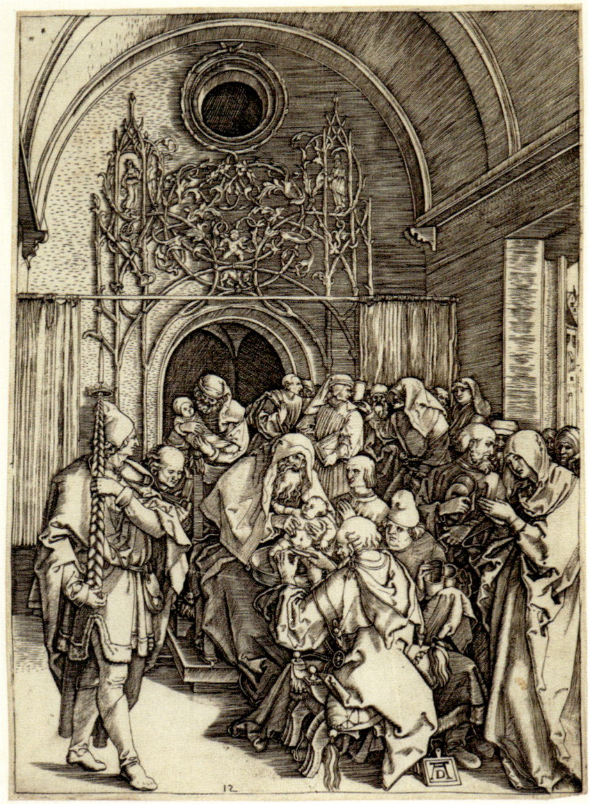

[Fig.8]
Albrecht Dürer,
The Circumcision, c.1504,
National Gallery of Scotland,
Edinburgh

[Fig.9]
Marcantonio Raimondi
(after Albrecht Dürer),
The Circumcision, c.1506,
National Gallery of Scotland,
Edinburgh

[Fig.10]
Anonymous artist
(after Albrecht Dürer),
The Circumcision, 1541(?),
National Gallery of Scotland,
Edinburgh

[Fig.11]
Hendrick Goltzius,
The Circumcision, 1594,
National Gallery of Scotland,
Edinburgh

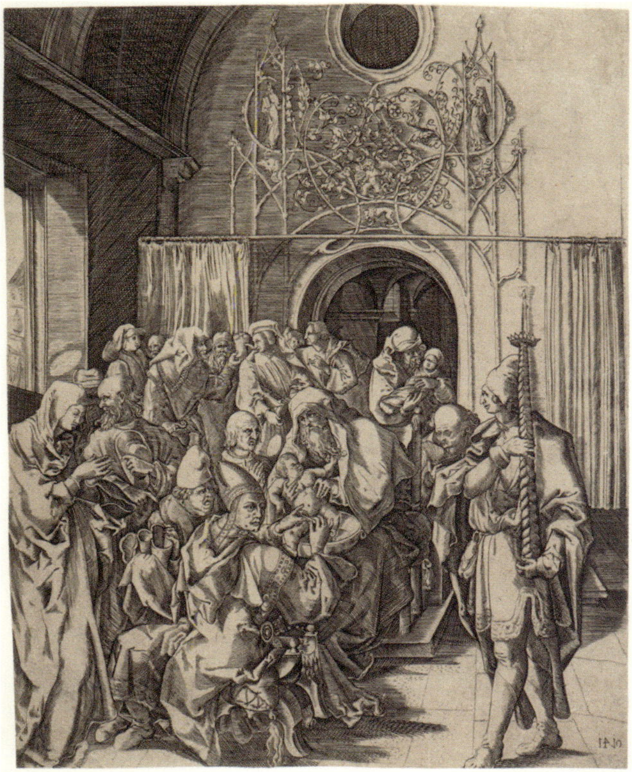

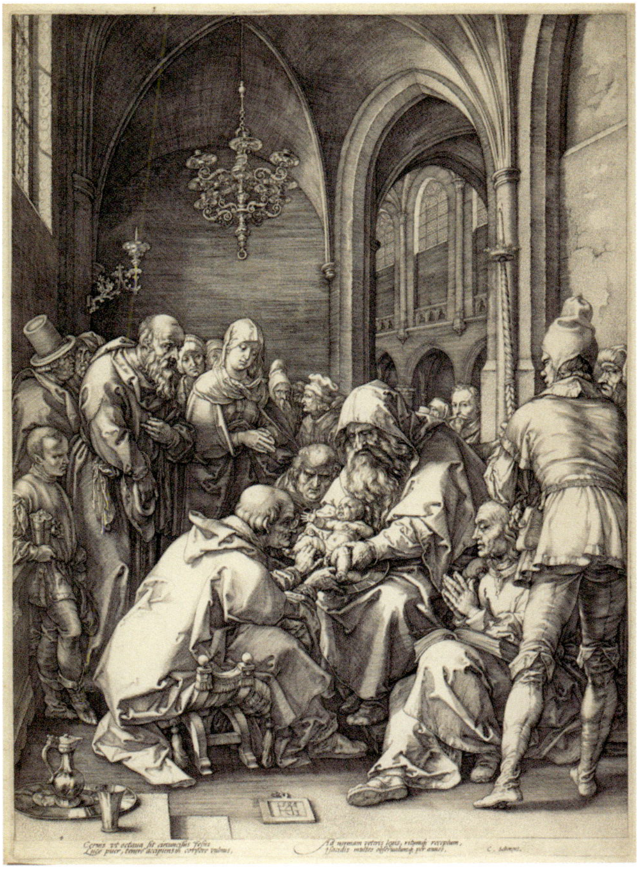

them accords with his preference for the grotesque, as is demonstrated in a number of his drawings of heads.[22] It is in the nature of a copy that, following the model, the copyist inevitably has to disguise his own identity to some extent in terms of style and technique. However, there are parallels in Ribera's work for the use of a broad pen and the hatching as seen here.[23] Moreover, the sketchy little figure holding a trident on top of the column particularly resembles similar creatures in Ribera drawings.[24]

At about the same time the Dutch painter Hendrick ter Brugghen modelled the central group of his large painting *The Beheading of Saint John the Baptist* on Dürer's woodcut of the same subject (fig.13).[25] The painting is now lost and only known from a workshop copy (fig.14). Ter Brugghen belonged to a group of painters known as the Utrecht Caravaggists who,

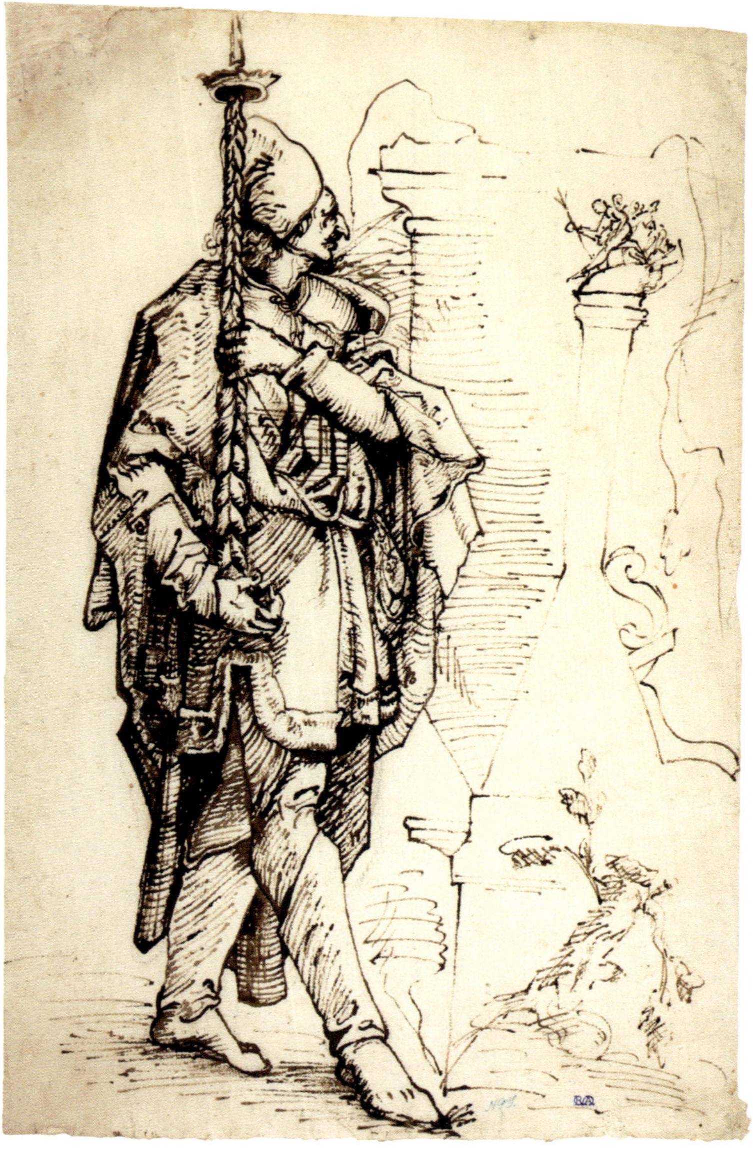

opposite [Fig.12]
Attributed to Jusepe de Ribera (after Albrecht Dürer), *Man Holding a Candlestick*, c.1620–30, National Gallery of Scotland, Edinburgh

[Fig.13]
Albrecht Dürer, *The Beheading of Saint John the Baptist*, 1510, The British Museum, London

[Fig.14] Workshop of Hendrick ter Brugghen, *The Beheading of Saint John the Baptist*, c.1620–30, National Gallery of Scotland, Edinburgh

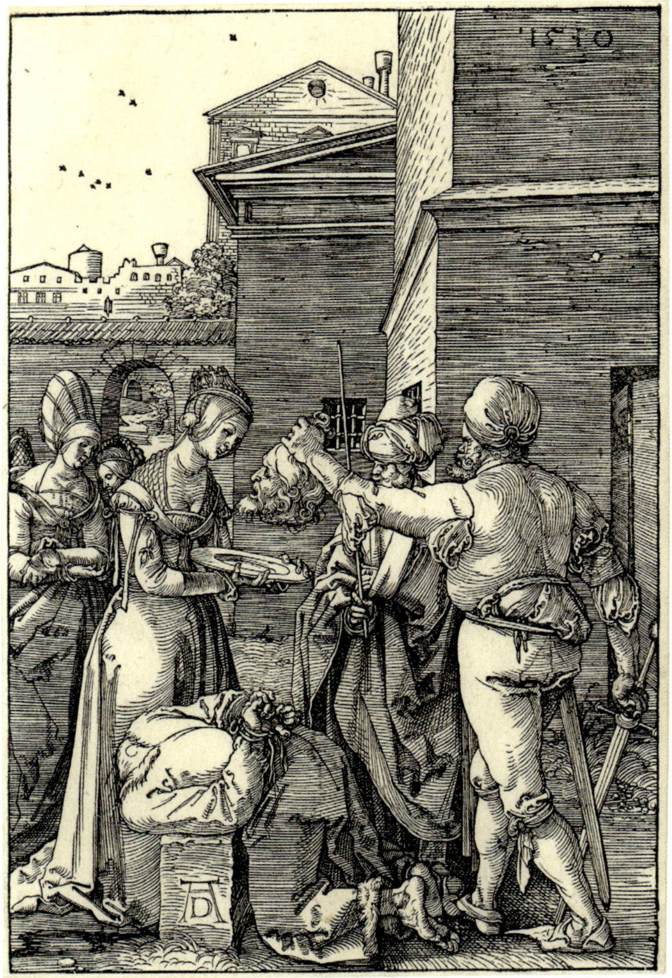

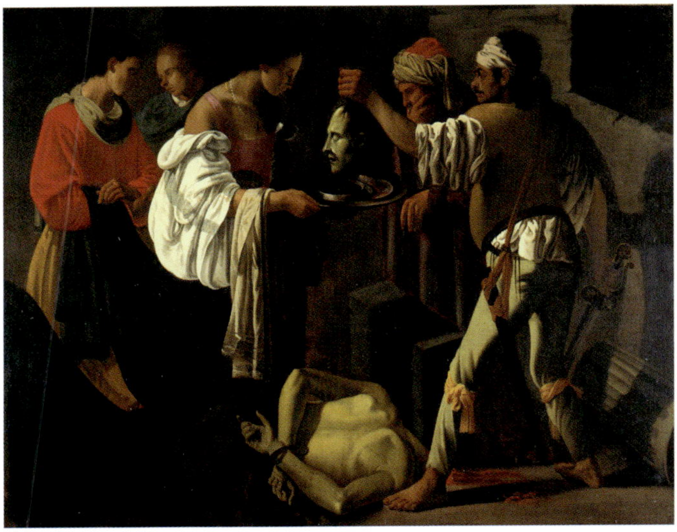

after working in Rome, brought Caravaggio's style to the Netherlands. Ter Brugghen frequently used prints by Dürer and Lucas van Leyden as sources for his compositions. The drawing attributed to Ribera and the composition by Ter Brugghen demonstrate the enormous importance of Dürer's prints as sources of inspiration for artists across Europe in the seventeenth century.

FAME PURCHASED: COLLECTING

Dürer was very successful at marketing his prints and always kept a keen eye on his profit. In a letter of 1509 to the wealthy Frankfurt burgher Jakob Heller, for whom he had painted an altarpiece, *The Coronation of the Virgin*, Dürer complained about the price being much too low in consideration of the time and material spent on it and he concluded: 'So henceforth I shall stick to my engraving, and had I done so before I should today have been a richer man by 1,000 florins.'[26] While this was probably an exaggeration, recent estimates have shown that the profit margin Dürer obtained from selling his prints was exceptionally good. He probably sold his woodcuts at around six times, and his engravings at an amazing twenty times, their production costs. For the distribution of his prints Dürer relied on travelling agents operating internationally, while his mother and wife sold them at fairs in Nuremberg and Frankfurt.[27] His stock was wide-ranging from small devotional prints to his expensive large format series. In 1511 Dürer published a second edition of *The Apocalypse* with a Latin text. And, in the same year he published *The Life of the Virgin*, *The Large Passion* and *The Small Passion* accompanied by distinguished Latin verses written by the humanist Benedictus Chelidonius. These books were innovative, highly sophisticated products for humanist devotion aiming at learned and wealthy clients.[28]

On his journey to the Netherlands from 1520 to 1521, Dürer exchanged, sold, and gifted a large number of his prints.[29] Among them were at least thirteen sets of *The Life of the Virgin*, fifteen impressions of *Saint Jerome in his Study* (fig.1), and six of his *Saint Anthony Reading* (fig.15).[30] In Antwerp he finally met the Dutch painter and printmaker Lucas van Leyden. In exchange for a set of Van Leyden's engravings, Dürer gave the artist some of his own prints, the total value of which he estimated at eight florins.[31] By way of comparison, the Nuremberg city apothecary and schoolmasters had an annual income of fifty to sixty florins. In 1509 Dürer bought his house there for 275 florins, and on his death his estate was estimated at almost 7,000 florins, which placed his family among the richest one hundred in Nuremberg.[32]

Little is known about the early collecting of Dürer's prints.[33] Certainly, they were kept in artists' workshops and humanists' libraries, and it is likely that Dürer's humanist friends Willibald Pirckheimer and Konrad Peutinger owned his graphic work. Ferdinand Columbus, son of the renowned explorer Christopher Columbus, had a large collection of prints, now dispersed, among them many by Dürer. He may even have met the artist in 1520 in the Netherlands.[34] The oldest albums of Dürer prints preserved intact belonged to Archduke Ferdinand II of Tyrol and were collated around 1560.[35] While there is no doubt that Dürer's fame did not fade after his death and his prints were in constant demand, around 1600 his reputation received another boost. This period was dominated by two intensely competitive collectors of Dürer's art, Duke (as of 1623, Prince Elector) Maximilian I of Bavaria in Munich and Emperor Rudolf II in Prague. Their insatiable appetite for works by Dürer and their appreciation of his style and technique triggered what has been called the 'Dürer Renaissance'.[36] Apart from Dürer's own work, there was also a focus on copies and imitations as well as creations in the master's style. Dürer gained an almost divine status, most obvious in Georg Vischer's *Christ and the Adulteress* (fig.16) of 1637, in which Christ's image is modelled on Dürer's famous *Self-portrait* of 1500 (Alte Pinakothek, Munich).[37] In 1609 the engraver and geographer Matthias Quad von Kinckelbach wrote that the obsessive veneration of Dürer's art had given it the status of holy relics.[38]

In Antwerp, Hieronymus and Johannes Wierix produced more than fifty engravings after Dürer prints. Their copies are masterpieces in their own right and consequently, in addition to Dürer's monogram, most of them bear marks that identify the engraver.[39] Johannes Wierix's faithful *Melencolia I* of 1602 (illustrated on page 6) is inscribed at the bottom

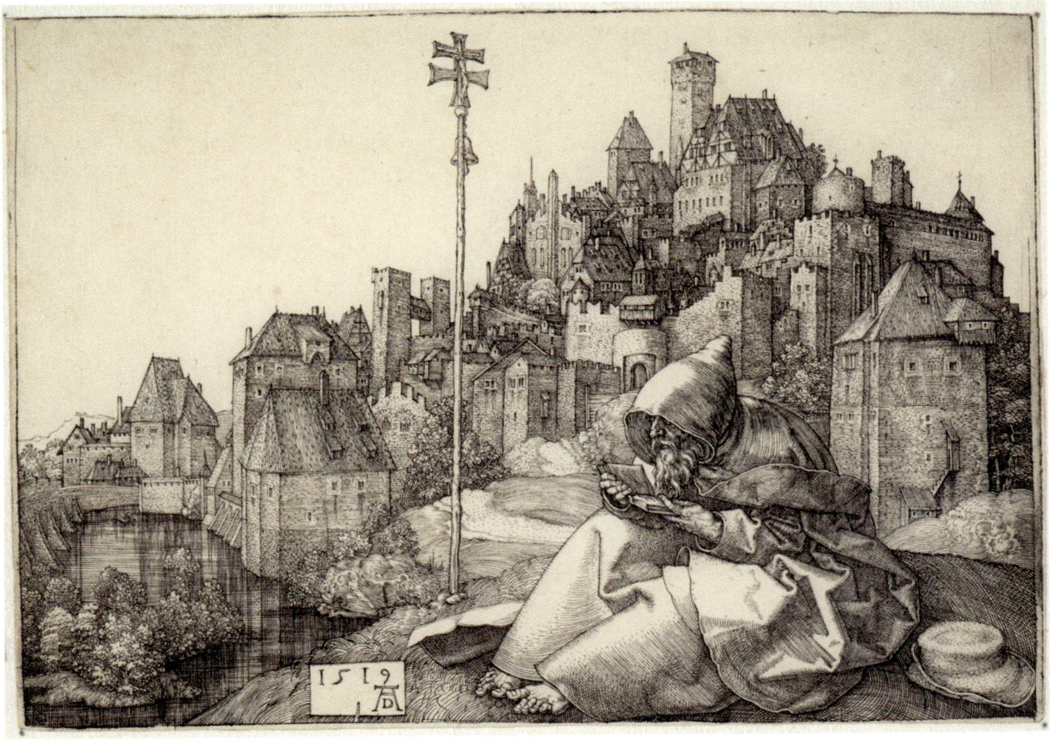

[Fig.15] Albrecht Dürer, *Saint Anthony Reading*, 1519, National Gallery of Scotland, Edinburgh

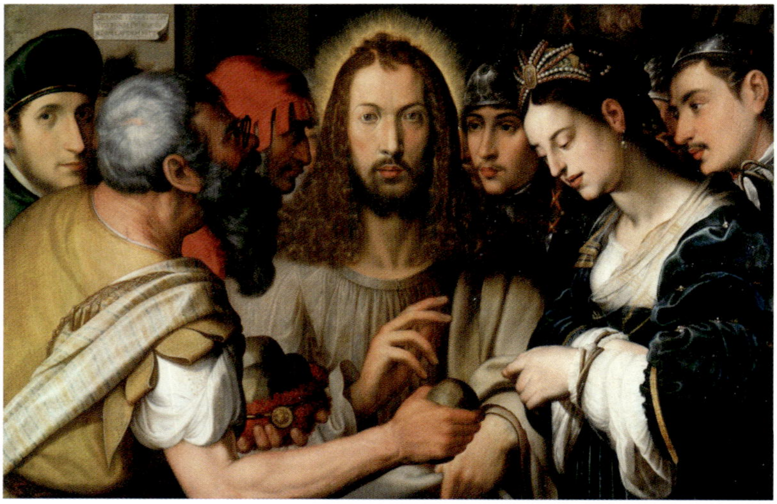

[Fig.16] Georg Vischer, *Christ and the Adulteress*, 1637,
Alte Pinakothek, Bayerische Staatsgemäldesammlungen, Munich

just outside the image. Obviously, it was all too tempting to trim these impressions and sell them as genuine Dürers. The work on display in the exhibition has escaped this fate and shows the inscription, but another in the collection has been 'Dürerised'. While the Wierix brothers were copying Dürer's prints and challenging his virtuosity, others went further. *The Entombment of Christ* by an anonymous (Augsburg?) engraver is stylistically and technically very close to Dürer's work (fig.17). This imitation bears an 'AD' monogram and the date 1507, but it is more likely to have been produced around 1600, a dating supported by the tablet with the inscription which shows strapwork ornaments fashionable at this time.

The demand for Dürer prints had other implications. After Dürer's death his widow and his brother Endres probably continued to print from the original copper plates and woodblocks. However, following Endres' death in 1555 the plates and woodblocks were dispersed. Little is known about their further history and only two plates have survived to the present day, although a number of woodblocks are still in existence.[40] Plates were collectors' items but they were also a precious production means for print publishers. Both aspects are reflected in the history of three copper plates and thirty-three woodblocks (along with some 3,000 prints probably pulled from these after 1600) from the estate of Gommer Spranger which were auctioned in 1638 in Amsterdam. They are most likely to have been collected by Bartholomäus Spranger, court painter to Emperor Rudolf II in Prague and Gommer's uncle. Cornelis Danckerts an eminent Amsterdam publisher bought twenty-four of the woodblocks, including the complete set for *The Life of the Virgin*.[41] These still feature in the 1667 inventory of his son, Dancker Danckerts who also possessed the copper plate of Johannes Wierix's *Melencolia I*.[42]

Plates and blocks continued to be used into the nineteenth century although constant use diminished their quality. Late impressions are mere ghosts but were still regarded as Dürer prints and sold and collected (fig.18). Moreover, even heavily damaged impressions were not thrown away but painstakingly restored, as can be demonstrated by the repairs visible on the reverse of an impression of the *The Sea Monster* (figs 19, 20). Sometimes the worn plates were reinforced or the damaged parts of the woodblocks were re-cut and reinserted. An example of this, but one which appears not to have been recognised by scholars, is Dürer's woodcut *Saint Jerome in a Cave* (fig.21). Two states of the same block have been recorded, one with the date 1512 and a later one with the date removed. The impression illustrated here is dated 1512. On close inspection, however, it turns out that it is not a first state impression, which would have the numbers of the date level. Instead, the numbers slope down slightly to the right indicating an undescribed state with the date re-cut and reinserted into the original block. This is probably due to the woodblock having been damaged through heavy use as it was also used as a title page for a book in 1514. The watermark of the present sheet suggests a dating of around 1563 to 1565. Comparisons show that the print in the National Galleries'

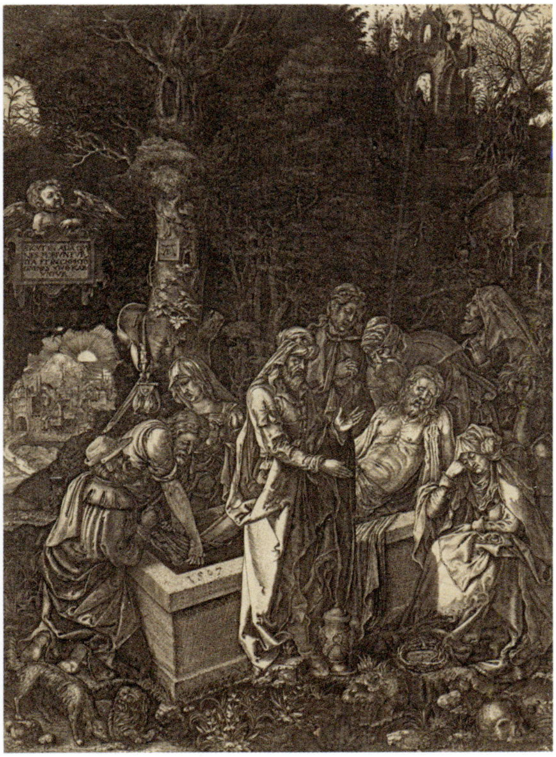

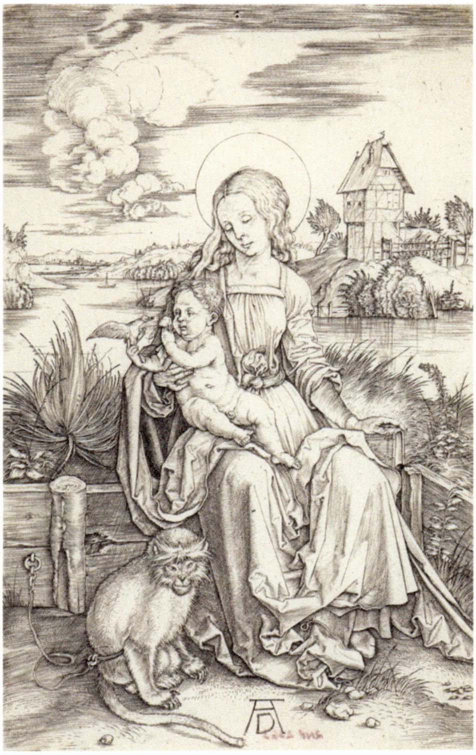

[Fig.17] Anonymous German (Augsburg?) artist, *The Entombment of Christ*, c.1600, National Gallery of Scotland, Edinburgh

[Fig.18] Albrecht Dürer, *Virgin and Child with a Monkey*, c.1498, National Gallery of Scotland, Edinburgh

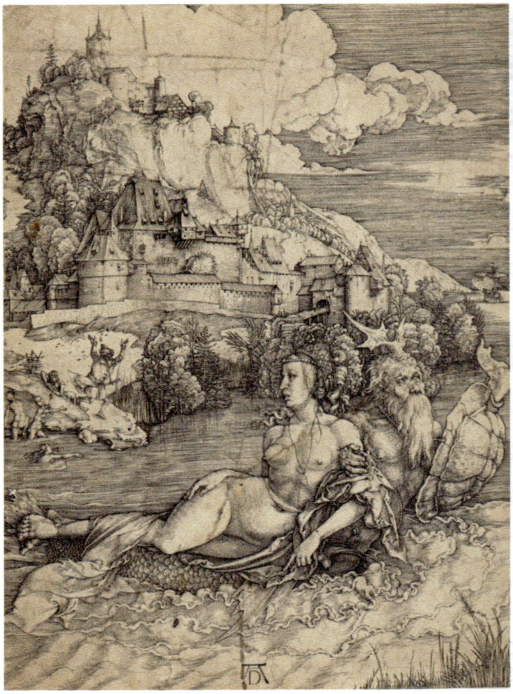

[Fig.19] Albrecht Dürer, *The Sea Monster (Das Meerwunder)*, verso, *c*.1498, National Gallery of Scotland, Edinburgh

[Fig.20] Albrecht Dürer, *The Sea Monster (Das Meerwunder)*, *c*.1498, National Gallery of Scotland, Edinburgh

collection does not show the typical damages of the final undated state, most prominently a large gap in the horizon. Thus, the replacement of the date, as shown in the impression on display, must have taken place before the date was finally abandoned. The present edition is the second state while the one without a date is the third.[43]

DÜRER'S FAME IN BRITAIN

The impression of Dürer's *Saint Jerome in a Cave* (fig.21) once belonged to Sir Joshua Reynolds. Although Reynolds's large and important collection contained a number of prints and even some drawings by Dürer, the German master had little appeal for him. Reynolds was not unusual in this respect as during the seventeenth and eighteenth centuries Italian and French art provided the standards by which artistic success was measured. The majority of British artists and art theorists despite recognising his consummate technical skills dismissed Dürer's works as hard and without grace. Moreover, he was accused of sticking to his own rules, that is his own treatises on proportion and perspective, rather than following nature and inspiration.[44] Positive remarks such as the one in a manuscript by the limner Nicholas Hilliard in 1602 that 'dowbtles he was the most

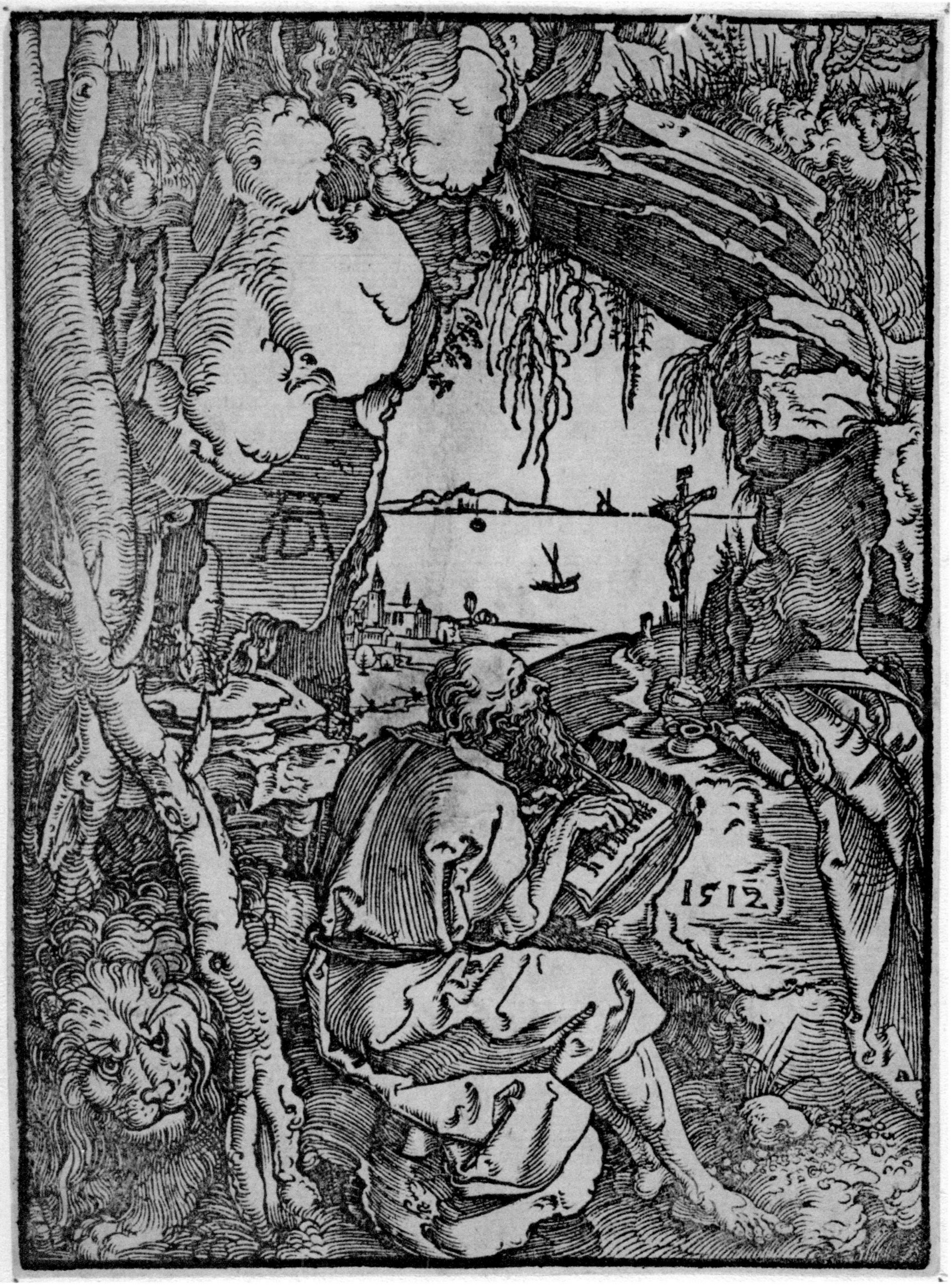

[Fig.21] Albrecht Dürer, *Saint Jerome in a Cave*, 1512, National Gallery of Scotland, Edinburgh

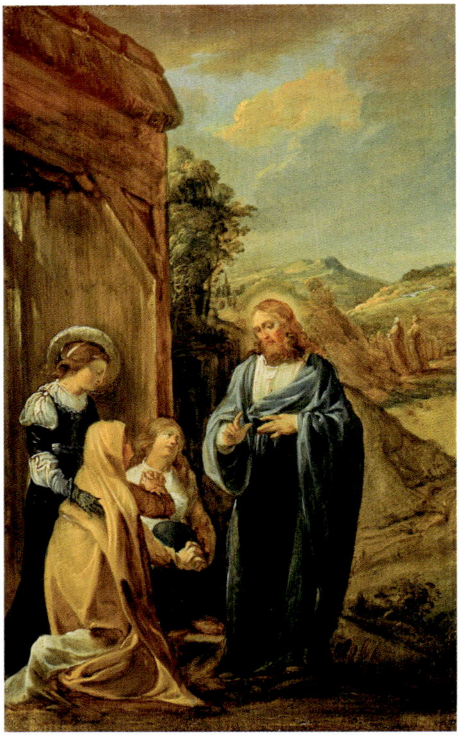

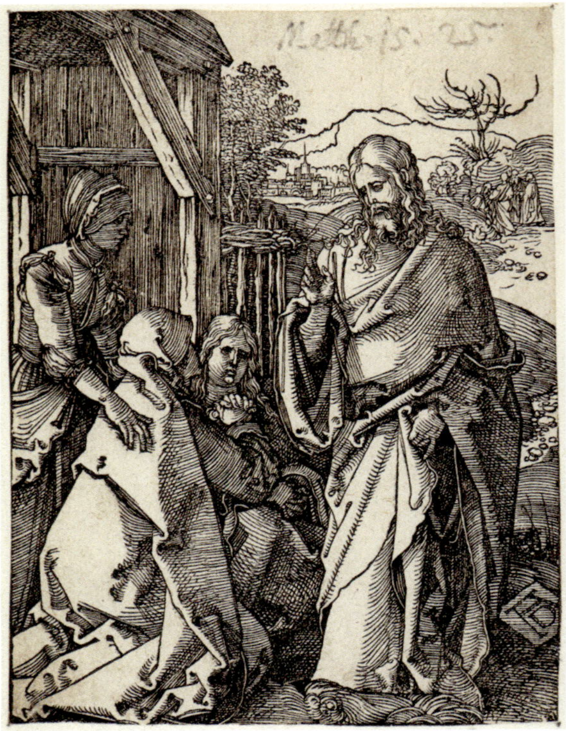

[Fig.22] John Runciman (after Albrecht Dürer), *Christ Taking Leave of his Mother*, c.1765, National Gallery of Scotland, Edinburgh

[Fig.23] Albrecht Dürer, *Christ Taking Leave of his Mother*, c.1508–9, National Gallery of Scotland, Edinburgh

exquisite man that euer leaft vs lines to vieue for true delineation' are rather rare, most comments refer to Dürer's brilliant technique, and are usually embedded in wider criticism of his art.[45] John Evelyn in his *Sculptura, or the History and Art of Chalcography* of 1662 called Dürer a 'prodigy of science' and rather exceptionally praised his 'wonders both in copper and wood' for their 'true and steady design, the incomparable proportion, and the stroke of his graver'.[46] William Gilpin in his *Essay upon Prints* of 1768 found Dürer's prints 'have great merit' and are 'so well executed'. He even conceded that 'this artist seems to have understood the principles of design. His composition is often pleasing; and his drawing generally good: but he knows very little about the management of light; and still less of grace.'[47] At about the same time John Runciman's small painting *Christ Taking Leave of his Mother* (fig.22) provides a surprising example of an artist using a design by Dürer as his compositional model. His small panel closely follows a Dürer woodcut of this subject from the series *The Small Passion* (fig.23). John Runciman, who died in Rome aged twenty-four, was the younger brother of the Scottish painter Alexander Runciman. John would have had access to old master prints from his brother's collection and presumably his little panels, which are also exceptional in mid-eighteenth century Scottish art for their Biblical subjects, were aesthetic experiments re-interpreting the prints. His painting *The Beheading of Saint John the Baptist* is based on the same Dürer woodcut (fig.13) Ter Brugghen had used 150 years earlier.[48] Even Reynolds, although not enamoured by the artist, had admitted that Dürer's prints offered 'a mass of genuine materials.'[49]

Dürer's reputation with British patrons and collectors was much more positive and although he had never crossed the Channel he had some English clients on the Continent.[50] Within the artist's lifetime Dirck Vellert whom Dürer had met in Antwerp, based his designs for stained glass windows in King's College Chapel in Cambridge on Dürer prints.[51] King Charles I and his friend Thomas Howard, Earl of Arundel were both enthusiastic collectors of works by Dürer. The famous *Self-portrait* of 1498 (Museo del Prado, Madrid) and the *Portrait of his Father* (National Gallery, London) were presented to Arundel in 1636 by the Nuremberg city council as gifts to Charles I. Before handing them over to the king, Arundel had copies made for his own collection.[52] In 1645 Wenceslaus Hollar made an etching after Arundel's copy of Dürer's *Self-portrait* (fig.24). Arundel, who was a keen print collector, was particularly interested in paintings and drawings by Dürer.[53] Richard Maitland, 4th Earl of Lauderdale brought together what probably was the most important print collection in Scotland in the seventeenth century. Maitland, a man of letters who had translated Virgil, was famous for his huge and exquisite library. In 1688 and 1689 he sold part of his collection at two auctions. The catalogues list more than 670 prints by Dürer.[54]

In addition to works by Dürer, portraits of the artist himself were in high demand. In 1629 the Antwerp printmaker Andries Stock made an engraving (fig.25) after Tommaso Vincidor's *Portrait of Albrecht Dürer*. In his diary Dürer noted that he met Vincidor in Antwerp in 1520. Vincidor, who had trained with Raphael, painted Dürer's portrait and intended to take it with him to Rome. Dürer gave him a full set of his prints for Raphael and wished to get Marcantonio Raimondi's prints after Raphael's designs in exchange.[55] Vincidor's painting (or a copy after it) seems to have entered Italy soon after as Vasari included Dürer's image in his early painting *Christ Carried to the Sepulchre* of 1532 (Casa Vasari, Arezzo).[56] Vincidor's painting is now lost but a copy after it, tentatively attributed to Sir Anthony van Dyck, was acquired in 1792 by the 5th Duke of Bedford and has been preserved at Woburn Abbey (fig.26).[57] This painting is possibly identical with or was copied from the one recorded in Willem van Haecht's painting of the Antwerp merchant Cornelis van der Geest's picture gallery, dated 1628 (Rubenshuis, Antwerp).[58]

It was not until the early nineteenth century that artists and writers joined collectors in Britain in almost unequivocally and openly praising Dürer's art.[59] Foundations for this had been laid by advancing connoisseurship and German Romanticism, which had a strong impact on British artists and collectors. It was Johann Heinrich Merck, a friend of the writer Goethe, who in two articles in 1780 and 1787 analysed the different quality of impressions and copies after Dürer's prints.[60] In 1797 Wilhelm Heinrich Wackenroder and Ludwig Tieck brought out their *Effusions from the Heart of an Art-Loving Monk* (*Herzensergießungen eines kunstliebenden Klosterbruders*), one of the most important manifestos of the early Romantic movement, which contained an essay on Dürer. The year after, Tieck published a novel *Franz Sternbald's Travels*.[61] The main character is the fictive painter Sternbald who trained in Dürer's workshop before setting out on his *Wanderjahre*. In the novel, Sternbald's meeting with Dürer in the Netherlands drew inspiration from Dürer's journal, first published in 1779. Wackenroder's and Tieck's writings had a strong impact on the Nazarenes, a group of German painters who sought to revive art based on late medieval, 'primitive' models. Romantic writers and artists, therefore, shaped the idealised image of Dürer as a diligent and pious, truly German, late-medieval artist. Connoisseurship culminated in Adam Bartsch's pioneering catalogue of old master prints published in twenty-one volumes from 1803 to 1821, and still used as a reference work. The volume on Dürer was first published in 1808. In 1828 the celebrations of the three-hundredth anniversary of Dürer's death involved huge numbers of artists and led to a massive popularisation of the artist's life and work.

It was on the back of this wave of expanded knowledge, artistic reverence, and popular acclaim that Dürer's fame in Britain reached its apogee. A crucial figure in this was the Scottish artist and writer William Bell Scott.[62] He had trained at the Trustees' Academy in Edinburgh with his father Robert who was an illustrator and engraver. Scott saw his father's

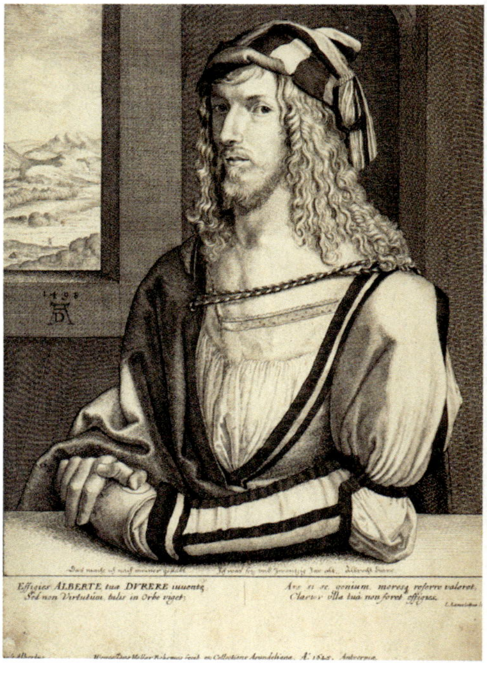

left to right

[Fig.24] Wenceslaus Hollar (after Albrecht Dürer), *Portrait of Albrecht Dürer*, 1645, Scottish National Portrait Gallery, Edinburgh

[Fig.25] Andries Jacobsz Stock (after Tommaso Vincidor), *Portrait of Albrecht Dürer*, 1629, Scottish National Portrait Gallery, Edinburgh

[Fig.26] Sir Anthony van Dyck, attributed to (after Tommaso Vincidor), *Portrait of Albrecht Dürer*, c.1622–7(?), Reproduced by kind permission of His Grace the Duke of Bedford and the Trustees of the Bedford Estates

workshop as 'the latest descendant of the mixed trade certainly carried on by Albert Dürer'.[63] In 1854 Scott travelled to Germany and visited Nuremberg during June and July. According to his memoirs, he painted *Albrecht Dürer in Nuremberg* (fig.27) on the balcony of the Dürer House.[64] A number of drawings from this tour survive in albums that were collated from 1861 onwards by Scott and his mistress Alice Boyd. Three drawings show imaginary scenes from Dürer's life set in the Dürer House.[65] Nuremberg was on the map of the British 'Northern Grand Tourists' and was praised in *The Art Journal* as 'fully worth a pilgrimage'.[66] A photograph of the Dürer House (fig.28) in an album, possibly assembled by the Glasgow chemist Walter Crum and his family, bears witness to its popularity and probably dates from as early as around 1860, making it one of the first known photographs of the house.[67] The photograph shows the balcony where Scott is supposed to have painted, before alterations were made in 1881.

William Bell Scott also made important contributions to Dürer scholarship. He drew attention to the unique volumes of sketches and manuscripts by Dürer which formed part of the London physician Hans Sloane's foundation bequest to the British Museum in 1753.[68] In 1869 Scott published the first Dürer monograph in English, including a complete catalogue of his works and a translation of the journal of his travel to the Netherlands.[69] Scott himself illustrated the book with etchings and woodcuts, some of which are copies after works by Dürer. He was also a keen collector of Dürer prints.[70] Scott was a friend and supporter of Dante Gabriel Rossetti who was a member of the Pre-Raphaelite brotherhood, a

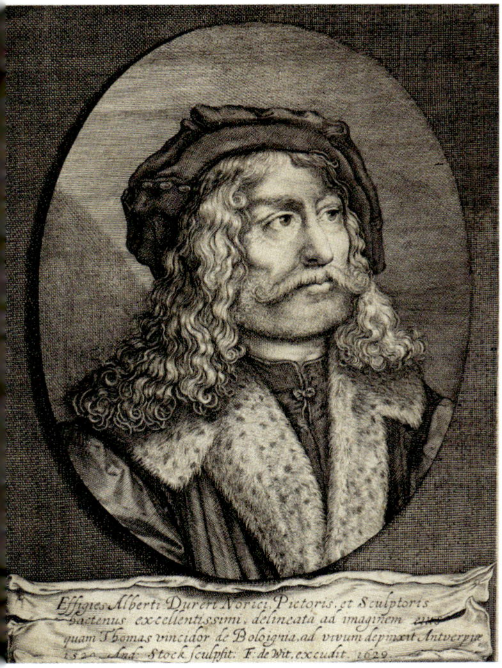

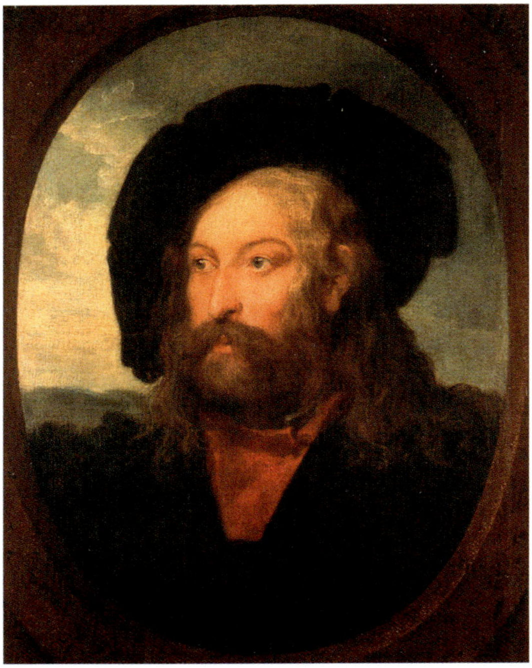

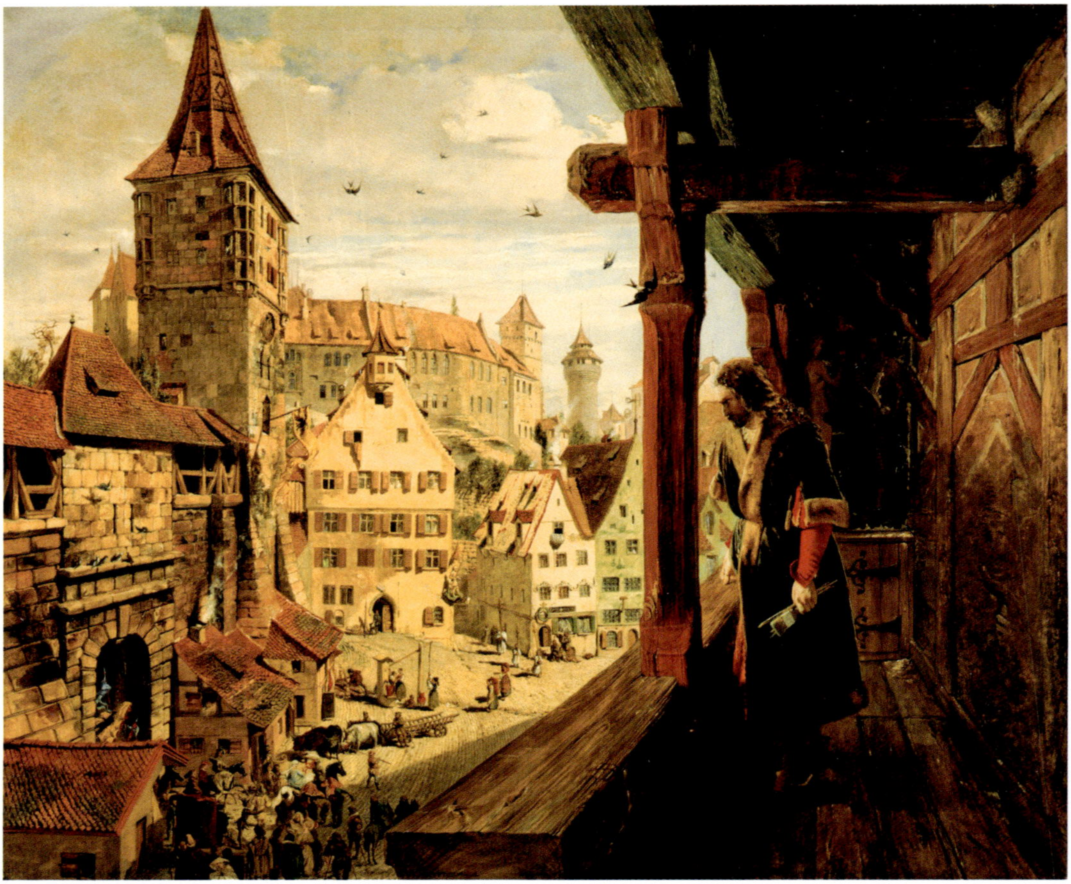

group of British artists who developed ideas similar to the Nazarenes and frequently took inspiration from prints by Dürer.[71]

The artist and critic Roger Fry's description of Dürer as 'the prince of craftsmen and consummate technician' encapsulated the qualities that made him a favourite of the Arts and Crafts movement towards the end of the nineteenth century.[72] In 1899 the Art Workers' Guild presented *Beauty's Awakening: A Masque of Winter and of Spring* at the Guildhall in London. Walter Crane, an artist and illustrator and a leading figure of the Arts and Crafts movement, chaired the organising committee and, in a costume he had designed himself, performed as Albrecht Dürer.[73] It was in this spirit that in the 1960s in the entrance hall of Glasgow School of Art, a mosaic portrait of Dürer was installed alongside one of the building's famous architect, Charles Rennie Mackintosh.

EPILOGUE: DÜRER'S FAME IN THE TWENTY-FIRST CENTURY

The veneration of Dürer and the mass reproduction of his artworks resulted in an extraordinary popularisation of the artist in the twentieth century, especially in Germany where Dürer has become a household name and is considered the ideal of a German artist. As such he was used by German nationalists and misused by Nazi propaganda.[74] Moreover, reproductions of his art became easily available and ubiquitous. Dürer's watercolours *The Hare* (fig.29) and *The Large Piece of Turf* (Albertina, Vienna) inspired Ottmar Hörl's installation *The Great Piece of Hares*. In 2003 Hörl transformed the Nuremberg market square into a lawn by using some 7,000 green plastic hares modelled on Dürer's watercolour (fig.30).[75] But, undoubtedly the most iconic of all Dürer's works is his *Study of Praying Hands* (fig.31). It has been endlessly reproduced and copied by amateur artists and has also found its way onto numerous devotional objects and into advertisements.[76] A producer of handball equipment recently issued a poster featuring the German handball international Pascal Hens (fig.32). He poses bare, showing the *Praying Hands* tattoo on his stomach, albeit in reverse. The mediums may have changed but the message remains: Dürer continues to inspire.

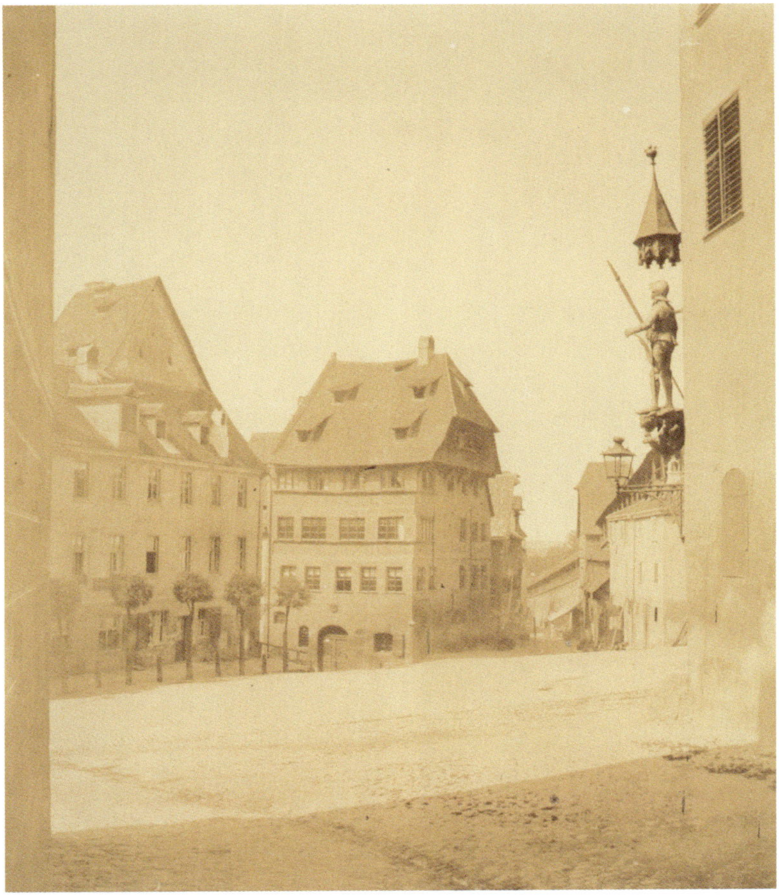

opposite [Fig.27] William Bell Scott, *Albrecht Dürer in Nuremberg*, 1854, National Gallery of Scotland, Edinburgh

above [Fig.28] Anonymous photographer, *The Albrecht Dürer House in Nuremberg*, c.1860s, Scottish National Portrait Gallery, Edinburgh

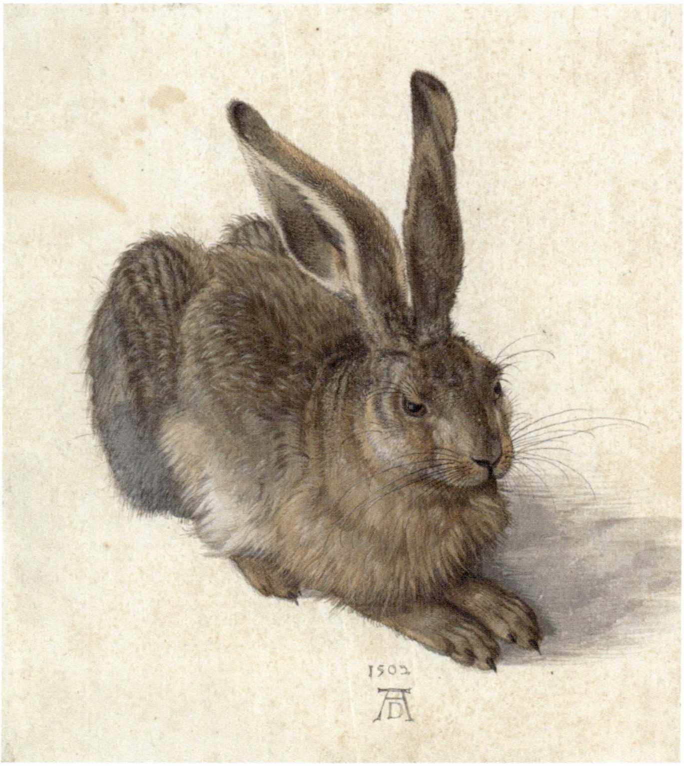

[Fig.29] Albrecht Dürer,
The Hare, 1502, Albertina, Vienna

opposite [Fig.30] Ottmar Hörl,
The Great Piece of Hares (*Das Große Hasenstück*), 2003
photo: Johannes Marburg

[Fig.31] Albrecht Dürer,
Study of Praying Hands, 1508, Albertir
Vienna

[Fig.32] Nilz Böhme (photographer
Portrait of Pascal Hens, 2006,
Private Collection

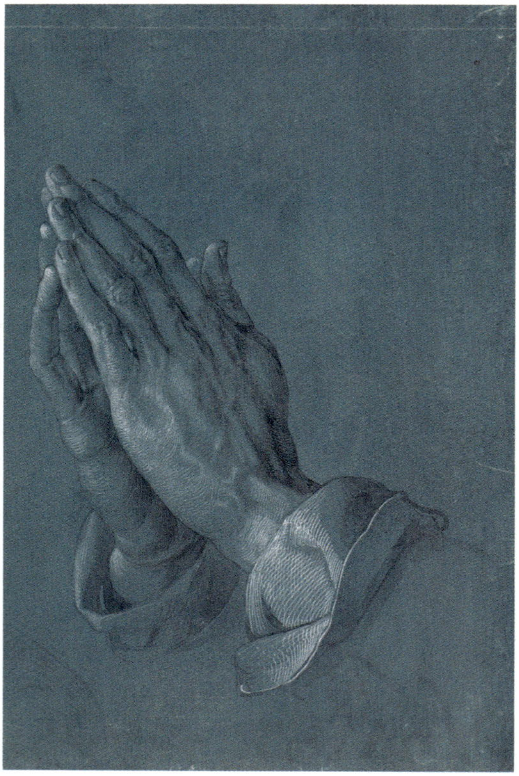

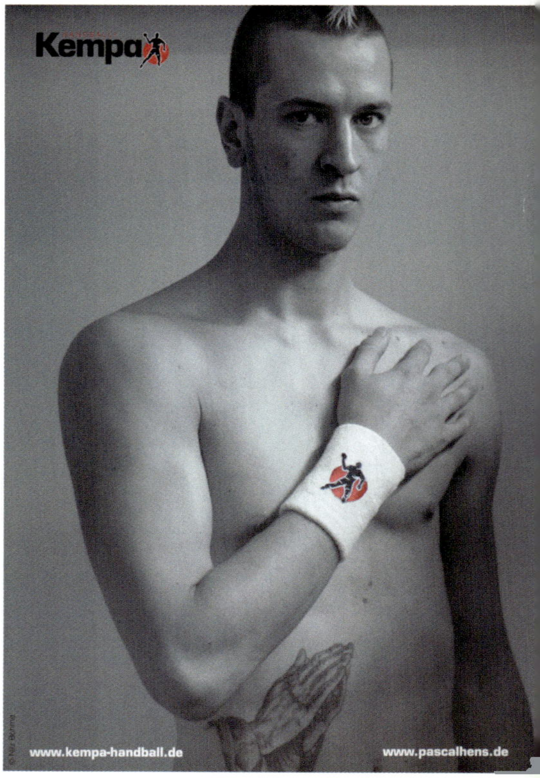

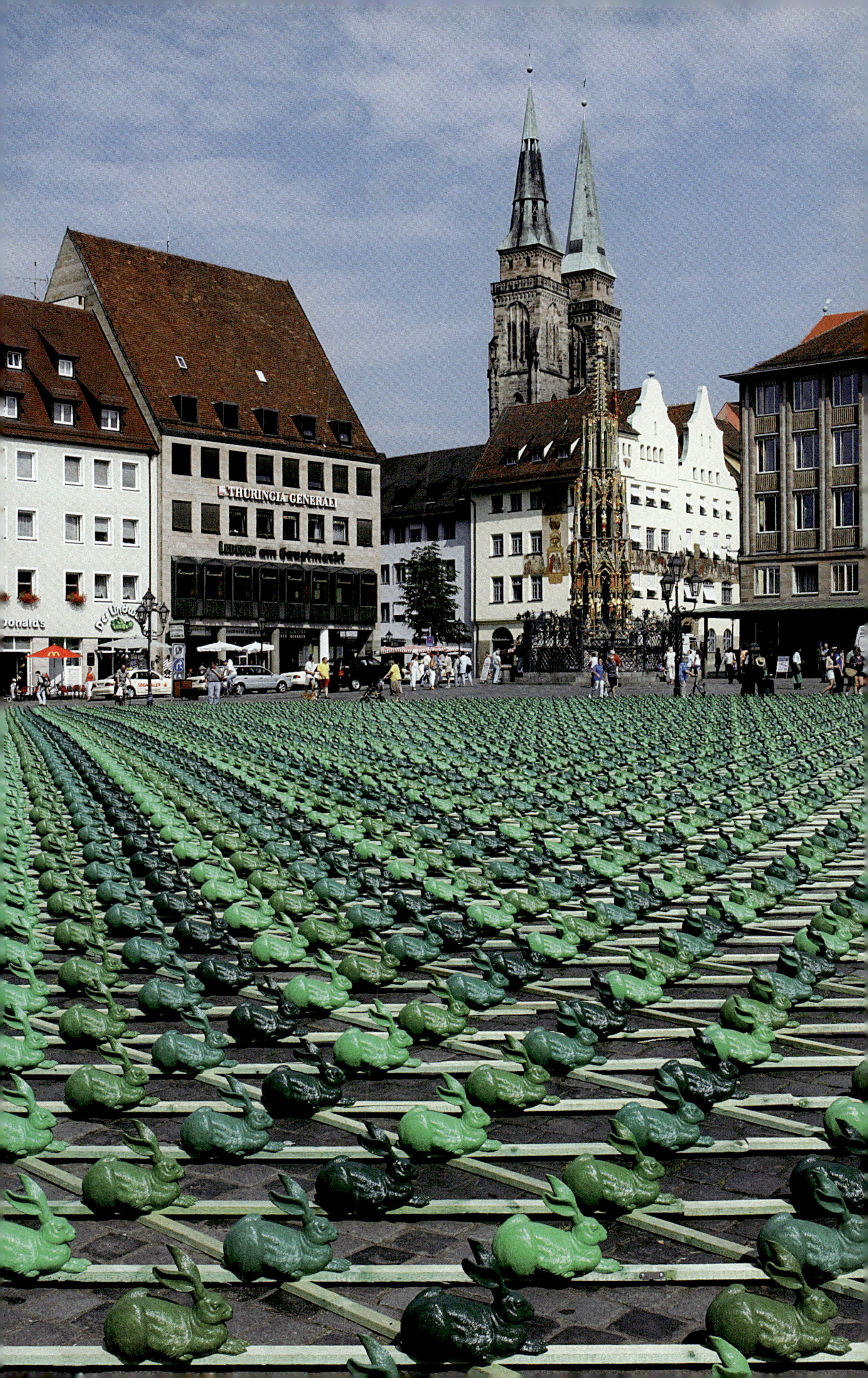
THURINGIA GENERALI

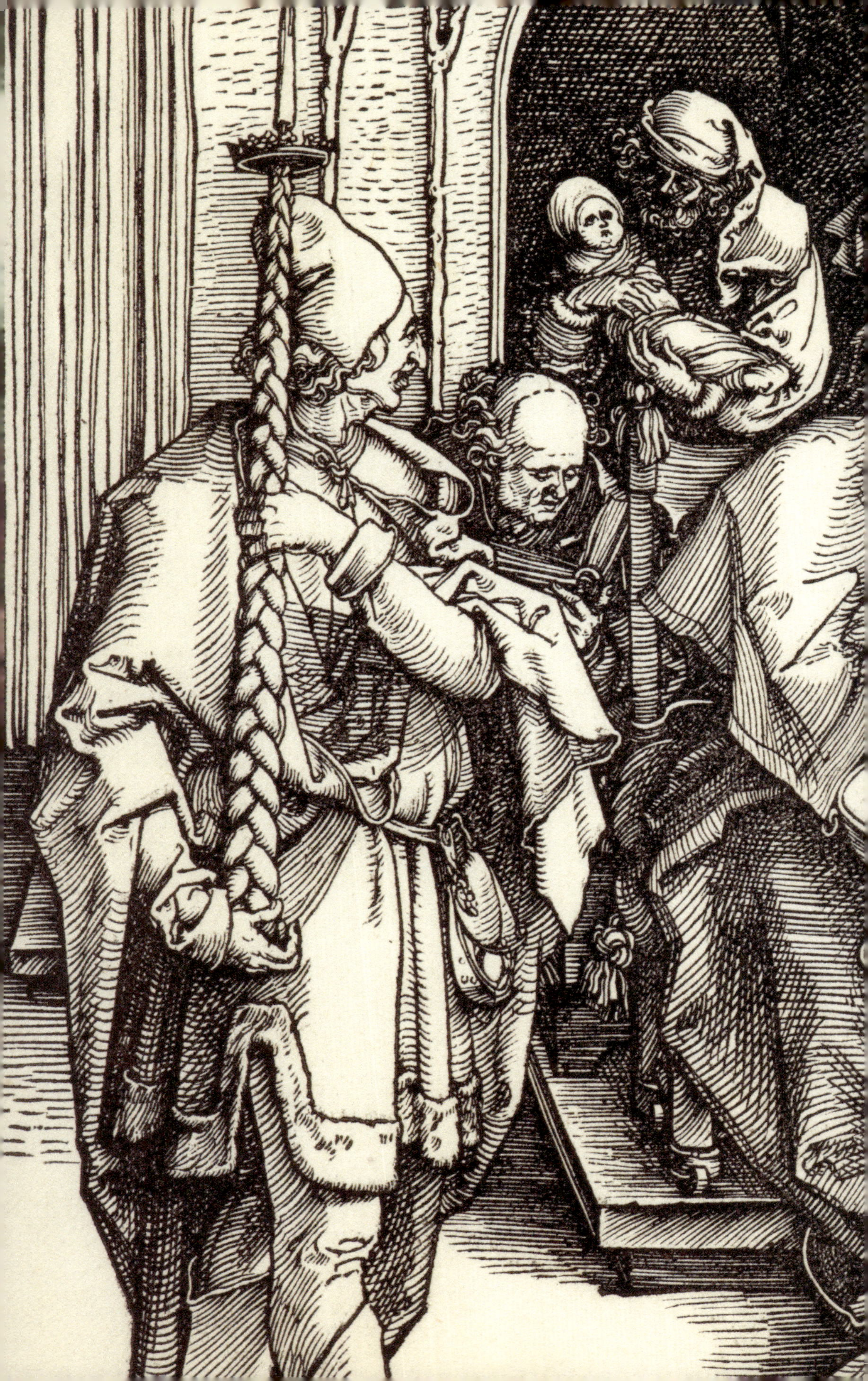

NOTES & REFERENCES

1. Białostocki 1986, p.31 (translation by Erwin Panofsky); Bartrum 2002, pp.11–12; for Erasmus's Latin text see Rupprich 1956, p.297.

2. For a tentative dating of 1496–7 for Dürer's first travel to Italy see G. Ulrich Großmann, 'Albrecht Dürer in Innsbruck. Zur Datierung der ersten italienischen Reise', in G. Ulrich Großmann and F. Sonnenberger (eds), *Das Dürer-Haus. Neue Ergebnisse der Forschung (Dürer-Forschungen I)*, Nuremberg 2007, pp.227–49, see also Katherine Crawford Luber, *Albrecht Dürer and the Venetian Renaissance*, Cambridge 2005, pp.40–76, who denies the first trip altogether.

3. Charles Talbot, 'Dürer and the High Art of Printmaking', in L. Silver and J.C. Smith (eds), *The Essential Dürer*, Philadelphia 2010, pp.35–61, especially p.50; Panofsky 1945, vol.1, pp.47–9.

4. Peter Parshall, 'German Renaissance Prints', in *Print Quarterly* 13 (1996), pp.197–200.

5. The author's translation; for Dürer's text see Rupprich 1956, p.151, for an English translation see Conway 1958, p.96.

6. O. ter Kuile, *Rijksmuseum Twenthe Enschede: Catalogus van schilderijen*, Enschede 1976, no.139, fig.187. With thanks to Lars Hendrikman and Paul Knolle.

7. On copies after Dürer's prints see Williamstown 1975 and Nuremberg 1978. On Dürer's impact during the sixteenth century see Koerner 2002, on his artistic reception see Nuremberg 1976, on Dürer and sculpture see H. Beck and P.C. Bol (eds), *Dürers Verwandlung in der Skulptur zwischen Renaissance und Barock*, exhibition catalogue, Frankfurt 1981.

8. For these see Vogt 2008, for his impact on Italian art in the sixteenth century see László Mészáros, *Italien sieht Dürer: Zur Wirkung der deutschen Druckgraphik auf die italienische Kunst des 16. Jahrhunderts (Erlanger Studien 48)*, Erlangen 1983 and Giovanni Maria Fara, *Albrecht Dürer: Originali, copie, derivazioni (Gabinetto Disegni e Stampe degli Uffizi: Inventario generale delle stampe 1)*, Florence 2007.

9. Vogt 2008, pp.139–43, no.1.

10. Vasari, vol.5, p.405.

11. *...si convenne con Marcantonio Bolognese di mandar fuori insieme queste carte.*, Vasari, vol.5, p.403; see Pon 2004, pp.139–40.

12. Norberto Gramaccini and Hans Jakob Meier, *Die Kunst der Interpretation: Italienische Reproduktionsgrafik 1485–1600*, Berlin and Munich 2009, pp.28–30, 80–1.

13. Williamstown 1975, pp.31–3. For a proof state of this print without any marks see Pon 2004, p.62, fig.30. With thanks to Michael Bury.

14. Pon 2004, pp.70–3. Landau attributes this series to Agostino Veneziano, see David Landau and Peter Parshall, *The Renaissance Print 1470–1550*, New Haven and London 1994, p.389, n.139. The only copy attributed to Raimondi bearing Dürer's monogram and made after 1510 is *Christ Appearing to Saint Gregory*, dated 1511 (B.644).

15. Koerner 2002, p.25, on Dürer and copyright see Vogt 2008, pp.77–94, and for the German text of the Nuremberg document see Rupprich 1956, p.241, no.4.

16. Giovanni Maria Fara, 'Sul secondo soggiorno di Albrecht Dürer in Italia e sulla sua amicizia con Giovanni Bellini', in *Prospettiva* 85 (January 1997), pp.91–6.

17. Red chalk, metal point, 40.3 × 28.3 cm, Albertina, Vienna, inv.no.17575; Achim Gnann, *The Era of Michelangelo: Masterpieces from the Albertina*, exhibition catalogue, Vienna, Venice and Bilbao 2004, no.34. On Dürer as a collector see Jeffrey Chipps Smith, 'Dürer as Collector', in *Renaissance Quarterly* 64 (2011), pp.1–49.

18. Vasari, vol.5, p.551.

19. Karel van Mander, *The Lives of the Illustrious Netherlandish and German Painters*, H. Miedema (ed.), 6 vols, Doornspijk 1994–9, vol.1, p.396 (fol.284v.), p.397 (translation), vol.5, pp.204–5 (commentary).

20. *het Albert Duurse stuk van Goltzius*; Lawrence W. Nichols, 'Hendrick Goltzius: Documents and Printed Literature Concerning his Life', in R. Falkenburg, J.P. Filedt Kok, H. Leeflang (eds), *Goltzius-Studies: Hendrick Goltzius (1558–1617) [Nederlands Kunsthistorisch Jaarboek 42–43*

< detail of fig.8

(1991–2)], Zwolle 1993, pp.77–120, especially p.91.

21. I am grateful to Aidan Weston-Lewis who proposed the attribution to Ribera and provided references. This attribution was supported, albeit with some reservation, by Gabriele Finaldi (email 11 May 2010).

22. Madrid 1992, nos. D.4, D.5, D.6, D.40, ills.; Naples 2009, vol.2, no.3.16, ill.

23. Madrid 1992, nos. D.11, D.16, ills.; Naples 2009, vol.2, no.3.17, ill.

24. Madrid 1992, nos. D.41, D. 42, ills.; Naples 2009, vol.2, no.3.19, ill.

25. B.125; M.231; Sch.152. First noted by Hans Kauffmann, 'Albrecht Dürer in der Kunst und im Kunsturteil um 1600', in *Vom Nachleben Dürers: Beiträge zur Kunst der Epoche von 1550 bis 1650* (*Anzeiger des Germanischen Nationalmuseums 1940–1953*), Berlin 1954, pp.18–60, especially p.57, n.57.

26. Conway 1958, p.70; for Dürer's text see Rupprich 1956, p.72.

27. Unverfehrt 2007, pp.215–16.

28. On these books see David Hotchkiss Price, *Albrecht Dürer's Renaissance: Humanism, Reformation, and the Art of Faith* (Ph.D dissertation), Ann Arbor 2003, pp.133–65 and Arwed Arnulf, 'Dürers Buchprojekte von 1511: Andachtsbücher für Humanisten', in *Marburger Jahrbuch für Kunstwissenschaft* 31 (2004), pp.145–74.

29. Robert Grigg, 'Studies on Dürer's Diary of his Journey to the Netherlands: The Distribution of the Melencolia I', in *Zeitschrift für Kunstgeschichte* 49 (1986), pp.398–409.

30. Unverfehrt 2007, pp.211–13.

31. Rupprich 1956, p.175; Conway 1958, p.123.

32. Unverfehrt 2007, p.214.

33. Bubenik 2007, pp.74–86.

34. Mark P. McDonald, *The Print Collection of Ferdinand Columbus (1488–1539): A Renaissance Collector in Seville*, 3 vols, London 2004. On Columbus and Dürer see especially vol.1, p.155, pp.181–2.

35. Peter Parshall, 'The Print Collection of Ferdinand, Archduke of Tyrol', in *Jahrbuch der Kunsthistorischen Sammlungen in Wien* 78 (1982), pp.139–90, especially pp.140–1 and pp.144–9, nos.1–3.

36. Gisela Goldberg, 'Zur Ausprägung der Dürer-Renaissance in München', in *Münchner Jahrbuch der bildenden Kunst* 31 (1980), pp.129–75; Bernhard Decker, 'Im Namen Dürers: Dürer-Renaissance um 1600', in K. Löcher (ed.), *Retrospektive Tendenzen in Kunst, Musik und Theologie um 1600 : Akten des interdisziplinären Symposions, 30./31. März 1990 in Nürnberg* (*Pirckheimer-Jahrbuch* 6), Nuremberg 1991, pp.9–49; Bubenik 2007, pp.8–15.

37. Oil on panel, 69.8 × 109.5 cm, signed and dated 1637, Bayerische Staatsgemäldesammlungen, Munich, inv.no.1411; see Gisela Goldberg, *Dürer-Renaissance*, exhibition catalogue, Munich 1971, no.18.

38. Bartrum 2002, p.16; for the German text see Heinz Lüdecke and Susanne Heiland, *Dürer und die Nachwelt: Urkunden, Briefe, Dichtungen und wissenschaftliche Betrachtungen aus vier Jahrhunderten*, Berlin 1955, p.65.

39. Zsuzsanna van Ruyven-Zeman, *The Wierix Family: Introduction and Guide to the Catalogue* (*Hollstein's Dutch & Flemish Etchings, Engravings and Woodcuts 1450–1700, vol. 69*), Rotterdam 2004, pp.xv–xviii.

40. On the wood blocks see Walter L. Strauss, *Albrecht Dürer: Woodcuts and Wood Blocks*, New York 1979, pp.619–49.

41. Thomas Schauerte, 'Dürer und Spranger: Ein Autographenfund im Spiegel der europäischen Sammlungsgeschichte. Mit einer Transkription der Amsterdamer Auktionsliste vom Februar 1638', in *Mitteilungen des Vereins für Geschichte der Stadt Nürnberg* 93 (2006), pp.25–69, especially pp.47–51.

42. Jan van der Waals, *Prenten in de Gouden Eeuw: van kunst tot kastpapier*, exhibition catalogue, Rotterdam 2006, p.202. With thanks to Jaap van der Veen.

43. This state first described, however, as third in the sequence, in the dealers Craddock & Barnard's Catalogue 134 (1977), no.103.

44. Levey 1972, pp.158–61, see also Vey 1960 and Dörrbecker 1998. For Reynolds as a collector see Sam Smiles (ed.), *Sir Joshua Reynolds: The*

Acquisition of Genius, exhibition catalogue, Plymouth 2009, pp.102–58.

45. Philip Norman, 'Nicholas Hilliard's Treatise Concerning "The Art of Limning"', in *The Walpole Society* I (1911–12), pp.1–54; Vey 1960, p.158; Levey 1972, p.158.

46. John Evelyn, *Sculptura, or the History and Art of Chalcography*, London 1755 (first edition 1662), pp. 43, 45, 64; Vey 1960, p.167. With thanks to Michael Bury.

47. William Gilpin, *An Essay upon Prints*, London 1768, pp.65–8; Levey 1972, p.159; Dörrbecker 1998, p.36.

48. Oil on panel, 18.4 × 13.3 cm, National Gallery of Scotland, inv.no. NG 1005, for similar small experimental pictures by John Runciman see NG 648, NG 792, NG 793 and NG 2116. On John Runciman and these pictures see Duncan Macmillan, *Painting in Scotland: The Golden Age*, exhibition catalogue, Edinburgh and London 1986, pp.43–50, nos 69–71, fig.29, col. pl. 13.

49. Joshua Reynolds, *Discourses on Art*, R.R. Wark (ed.), New Haven and London 1997, p.108; Dörrbecker 1998, p.37.

50. Levey 1972, pp.157–8.

51. Hilary G. Wayment, 'The Use of Engravings in the Design of the Renaissance Windows of King's College Chapel, Cambridge', in *Burlington Magazine* 100 (1958), pp.378–8.

52. Susan Foister, 'Dürer's Nuremberg Legacy: The Case of the National Gallery portrait of Dürer's Father', in G. Bartrum (ed.), *Albrecht Dürer's Legacy*, conference held on 21 March 2003 at the British Museum, London. For the papers see *http://www.britishmuseum.org/research/research_publications/online_publications/durer_and_his_legacy.aspx*

53. David Howarth, *Lord Arundel and his Circle*, New Haven and London 1985.

54. Benjamin Walford, *Catalogus librorum instructissimae bibliothecae nobilis cujusdam Scoto Britani...* [Richard Maitland sale, 30 October 1688], London 1688, p.156, lot 71 ('An entire Collection of the Works of A'bert. Durer, containing Two Hundred and Twenty Prints') and Benjamin Walford, *Pinacotheca Maitlandiana: or a Catalogue of the Lord Maitland's Prints and drawings...* [sale 20 January 1689], London 1689, pp. 4, 7, 9, 11–12, 14, lots 28–31, 134, 210, 267–77, 284, 333, 339, 355. With thanks to Robert Ferguson and Robert Wenley. On Richard Maitland see Robert Douglas, *The Scots Peerage*, 9 vols, Edinburgh 1904–14, vol.5, pp.309–10, on his collection see John Lawler, *Book Auctions in England in the Seventeenth Century (1676–1700)*, London 1898, pp.169–75.

55. Rupprich 1956, p.158; Conway 1958, pp.105–6.

56. Sharon Gregory, 'Vasari's early interest in Dürer: 'Un nordico ritratto' in *Christ carried to the Sepulchre*', in *Apollo* 141 (March 1995), pp.33–5.

57. Susan J. Barnes, Nora de Poorter, Oliver Millar and Horst Vey, *Van Dyck: A Complete Catalogue of the Paintings*, New Haven and London 2004, no.II.41. With thanks to Kristin Lohse Belkin.

58. Ariane van Suchtelen and Ben van Beneden, *Room for Art in Seventeenth-Century Antwerp*, exhibition catalogue, The Hague and Antwerp 2009, pp.67–74, 123, 128–9, no.10, fig.35. For a drawing attributed to Jan de Bisschop dated *c.*1660–70 after Vincidor's painting see Matthias Mende, *Albrecht Dürer: Ein Künstler in seiner Stadt*, exhibition catalogue, Nuremberg 2000, p.217, ill.

59. Levey 1972, pp.159–62; Finke 1976, pp.19–21.

60. Białostocki 1986, pp.147–60.

61. Białostocki 1986, pp.79–90.

62. Christian 1973, pp.57–60; Finke 1976, pp.27, 32–3; Białostocki 1986, pp.243–5.

63. Scott 1892, vol.1, p.45.

64. Scott 1892, vol.2, p.319–20.

65. The albums are kept in the National Gallery of Scotland, inv.nos D 4712–4715. Two of the Dürer scenes are in D 4714, fol.43v and another is in D 5535, unpaginated. A similar watercolour by Scott was sold at Sotheby's Belgravia, Glasgow, 16 December 1975, lot 67, ill.

66. *The Art Journal* NS 3 (1851), p.35; Finke 1976, pp.24–5.

67. For a woodcut of the house and its environments in the same situation, dated 1862 see Nuremberg 1991, p.28, fig.19. An unpublished photograph very similar to the one in the Crum album is in Graphische Sammlung der Stadt Nürnberg, inv.no.Gr.A.6159.

68. William Bell Scott, 'Manuscripts of Albrecht Dürer in the Library and Print-Room of the British Museum and elsewhere', in *The Art Journal* NS 7 (1861), pp.106–7. On Sloane's collection of prints and drawings see John Rowlands, 'Prints and Drawings', in A. MacGregor (ed.), *Sir Hans Sloane: Collector, Scientist, Antiquary – Founding Father of the British Museum*, London 1994, pp.245–62.

69. William Bell Scott, *Albert Dürer: His Life and Works*, London 1869. Scott's own copy with copious notes is kept in the British Library (shelfmark C.61.b.8), see Nuremberg 1991, p.30.

70. His collection of prints was sold at three auctions: Sotheby, Wilkinson & Hodge, London, 2 February 1870 (Dürer lots 58–79), 20–4 April 1885 (Dürer lots 302–75) and 14 July 1892 (Dürer lots 31–6, 67–9). With thanks to Helen Smailes.

71. Christian 1973.

72. Białostocki 1986, p.261.

73. *The Studio*, special summer number, London 1899, p.42, fig.28, see Matthias Mende, *Düreriana: Neuerwerbungen der Albrecht-Dürer-Haus Stiftung e.V. Nürnberg*, exhibition catalogue, Nuremberg 1991, no.63, ill.

74. Berthold Hinz, *Dürer's Gloria*, exhibition catalogue, Berlin 1971; Jane Campbell Hutchison, *Albrecht Dürer: A Biography*, Princeton 1990, pp.187–206; Ute Kuhlemann, 'The Celebration of Dürer in Germany during the Nineteenth and Twentieth Centuries', in London 2002, pp.39–60.

75. Ottmar Hörl, *Das Große Hasenstück/ The Great Piece of Hares: Eine Dokumentation zur Großskulptur von Ottmar Hörl auf dem Hauptmarkt in Nürnberg 2.8.-17.8.2003*, Darmstadt 2003.

76. Karin Wimmer, *Albrecht Dürers 'Betende Hände' und ihre trivialisierte Rezeption* (unpublished Ph.D dissertation), Innsbruck 1999.

ABBREVIATIONS & FURTHER READING

B.
Adam Bartsch, *Le peintre graveur*, 21 vols, Vienna 1803–1821

BARTRUM 2002
Giulia Bartrum, 'Dürer Viewed by his Contemporaries', in London 2002, pp.9–17

BIAŁOSTOCKI 1986
Jan Białostocki, *Dürer and his Critics 1500–1971: Chapters in the History of Ideas. Including a Collection of Texts (Saecula Spiritalia 7)*, Baden-Baden 1986

BRIQUET
C.M. Briquet, *Les Filigranes: Dictionnaire historique des marques du papier*, 4 vols, Leipzig 1923

BUBENIK 2007
Andrea S. Bubenik, *The Reception of Albrecht Dürer in Central Europe, 1528–1700: Aspects of Art, Science and Collecting* (Ph.D dissertation), Kingston (Ontario) 2007

CHRISTIAN 1973
John Christian, 'Early German Sources for Pre-Raphaelite Designs', in *The Art Quarterly* 36 (1973), pp.56–83

CHURCHILL
W.A. Churchill, *Watermarks in Paper*, Amsterdam 1935

CONWAY 1958
William Martin Conway (ed.), *The Writings of Albrecht Dürer*, London 1958

DÖRRBECKER 1998
Detlef W. Dörrbecker, 'Dürer in der britischen Kunstliteratur des späten 18. Jahrhunderts', *Anzeiger des Germanischen Nationalmuseums* 1998, pp.35–41

FINKE 1976
Ulrich Finke, *Französische und englische Dürer-Rezeption im 19. Jahrhundert (Renaissance Vorträge 4/5)*, Nuremberg 1976

HEAWOOD
Edward Heawood, *I. Watermarks: Mainly of the 17th and 18th Centuries (Monumenta Chartæ Papyraceæ)*, Hilversum 1950

KOERNER 2002
Joseph Koerner, 'Albrecht Dürer: A sixteenth-Century Influenza', in London 2002, pp.18–38

LEVEY 1972
Michael Levey, 'Dürer and England', in *Anzeiger des Germanischen Nationalmuseums* 1971/1972, pp.157–64

LONDON 2002
G. Bartrum (ed.), *Albrecht Dürer and his Legacy: The Graphic Work of a Renaissance Artist*, exhibition catalogue, London 2002

LUGT
Frits Lugt, *Les marques des collections de dessins et d'estampes*, Amsterdam 1921

M.
Joseph Meder, *Dürer-Katalog: Ein Handbuch über Albrecht Dürers Stiche, Radierungen, Holzschnitte, deren Zustände, Ausgaben und Wasserzeichen*, Vienna 1932

MADRID 1992
Alfonso E. Pérez Sánchez and Nicola Spinosa (eds), *Ribera 1591–1652*, exhibition catalogue, Madrid 1992

NAPLES 2009
Nicola Spinosa (ed.), *Ritorno al barocco: Da Caravaggio a Vanvitelli*, 2 vols, exhibiton catalogue, Naples 2009

NUREMBERG 1976
Matthias Mende, *Wirkung und Nachleben Dürers: Neuerwerbungen und Leihgaben der letzten Jahre (Ausstellungskataloge der Stadtgeschichtlichen Museen Nürnberg 9)*, exhibition catalogue, Nuremberg 1976

NUREMBERG 1978
Peter Strieder and Leonie von Wilckens (eds), *Vorbild Dürer: Kupferstiche und Holzschnitte Albrecht Dürers im Spiegel der europäischen Druckgraphik des 16. Jahrhunderts*, exhibition catalogue, Nuremberg 1978

NUREMBERG 1991
Matthias Mende, *Das Dürerhaus in Nürnberg: Geschichte und Gegenwart in Ansichten von 1714 bis 1990/The Dürer House in Nuremberg: Its Past and Present in Views from 1714 to 1990*, exhibition catalogue, Nuremberg 1991

PANOFSKY 1945
Erwin Panofsky, *Albrecht Dürer*, 2 vols, Princeton 1945 (1st edition 1943)

PON 2004
Lisa Pon, *Raphael, Dürer, and Marcantonio Raimondi: Copying and the Italian Renaissance Print*, New Haven and London 2004

RUPPRICH 1956
Hans Rupprich, *Dürer: Schriftlicher Nachlass*, vol.1 (of 3), Berlin 1956

SCH.
Rainer Schoch, Matthias Mende and Anna Scherbaum, *Albrecht Dürer: Das druckgraphische Werk*, 3 vols, Munich, London and New York 2001–4

SCOTT 1892
W. Minto (ed.), *Autobiographical Notes of the Life of William Bell Scott*, 2 vols, London 1892

UNVERFEHRT 2007
Gerd Unverfehrt, *Da sah ich viel köstliche Dinge: Albrecht Dürers Reise in die Niederlande*, Göttingen 2007

VASARI
Giorgio Vasari, *Le vite de' piu eccelenti pittori* (...), G. Milanesi (ed.), 9 vols, Florence 1906

VEY 1960
Horst Vey, 'Nicholas Hilliard und Albrecht Dürer', in H. Ladendorf and H. Vey (eds), *Mouseion: Studien aus Kunst und Geschichte für Otto H. Förster*, Cologne 1960, pp.155–68

VOGT 2008
Christine Vogt, *Das druckgraphische Bild nach Vorlagen Albrecht Dürers (1417–1528): Zum Phänomen der graphischen Kopie (Reproduktion) zu Lebseiten Dürers nördlich der Alpen (Aachener Bibliothek 6)*, Munich and Berlin 2008

WILLIAMSTOWN 1975
Dürer Through Other Eyes: His Graphic Work Mirrored in Copies and Forgeries of Three Centuries, exhibition catalogue, Williamstown (MA) 1975

EXHIBITION CHECKLIST

All works by Albrecht Dürer are in chronological order, followed by works by other artists in alphabetical order.

Albrecht Dürer (1471–1528)

The Holy Family with the Dragonfly, c.1495

Engraving 23.7 × 18.3 cm, no watermark
Verso: inscription in brown ink 'P. mariette 1670'
References: B.44; M.42 (a/b); Sch.2 (a/b)
Provenance: purchased (£100) by A. Maitland from Colnaghi's, London, 1921; Sir Alexander Maitland Bequest, 1965
DÜRER 67 (P 2670)

The Martyrdom of Saint John, c.1496–7

(from *The Apocalypse*; 2nd edition 1511, with Latin text on verso)
Woodcut 39 × 28.2 cm, no watermark
References: B.61; M.164; Sch.112
Provenance: purchased from Colnaghi's, London, 1965
DÜRER 47 (P2665 WHOLE SERIES) · FIG.3

The Beast with Two Horns like a Lamb, c.1496–7

(from *The Apocalypse* II; 2nd edition 1511, with Latin text on verso)
Woodcut, 39.2 × 28.2 cm, no watermark
References: B.74; M.175; Sch.123
Provenance: purchased from Colnaghi's, London, 1965
DÜRER 60 (P 2665 WHOLE SERIES)

Virgin and Child with a Monkey, c.1498

Engraving, 19.2 × 12.5 cm, no watermark
Verso: black stamp 'Dr Euscher' (framed) [not in Lugt]; in pencil 'meo.', '16f', '104', 'P/H'
References: B.42; M.30 (l); Sch.20 (l)
Provenance: Dr Euscher(?); George H. Liston-Foulis Bequest, Edinburgh, 1958
DÜRER 72 (P 2363) · FIG.18

The Sea Monster (Das Meerwunder), c.1498

Engraving, 25.2 × 19 cm, no watermark
Verso: S. Barden's stamps in black (Lugt 218, 2756)
References: B.71; M.66 (a/b); Sch.21 (a/b)
Provenance: Siegfried Barden (1854–1917); purchased from Colnaghi's, London, 1961
DÜRER 63 (P 2499)

The Sea Monster (Das Meerwunder), c.1498

Engraving, 25 × 18.6 cm, watermark similar to M.20
Verso: inscriptions in black ink 'Albert Durer/ Rape of Anynome/ 6^{10} Bartsch' and in pencil 'Albert Durer./ 6^{10} Bartsch/ Rape of Anynome'
References: B.71; M.66 (a/b); Sch.21 (a/b)
Provenance: presented by the Royal Scottish Museum, Edinburgh, 1952
DÜRER 64 (P 2173) · FIGS 19, 20

Nemesis (The Large Fortune), c.1501

Engraving, 33.3 × 23.2 cm, watermark similar to M.20
References: B.77; M.72 (2a/b); Sch.33 (2a/b)
Provenance: unknown
DÜRER 76 (FRONTISPIECE)

Nemesis (The Large Fortune), c.1501

Engraving, 32.6 × 22.8 cm; inscription in brown ink 'cosas.Alegres', watermark similar to Briquet 1883 (Florence 1529)
Verso: inscription in black ink 'paid for this Albrecht Dürer £1-15-0' and 'Cos'
References: B.77; M.72 (2c/d); Sch.33 (2c/d)
Provenance: purchased 1909
DÜRER 92 (P 72)

Adam and Eve, 1504

Engraving, 25 × 19.5 cm, watermark M.62
References: B.1; M.1 (3a); Sch.39 (3a)
Provenance: Sir Alexander Maitland Bequest, 1965
DÜRER 75 (P 2671)

The Circumcision, c.1504

(from *The Life of the Virgin*, II)
Woodcut, 29.6 × 21.1 cm, watermark similar to M.20
References: B.86; M.198 (before text, b); Sch.176 (before text, b)
Provenance: purchased from Colnaghi's, London, 1966
DÜRER 38 (P 2677 WHOLE SERIES) · FIG.8

The Flight into Egypt, c.1504

(from *The Life of the Virgin*, 14)
Woodcut, 30 × 21 cm, watermark M.56
References: B.89; M.201 (before text, a); Sch.179 (before text, a)
Provenance: purchased from Colnaghi's, London, 1966
DÜRER 26 (P 2677 WHOLE SERIES)

The Glorification of the Virgin, c.1502

(from *The Life of the Virgin*, 20)
Engraving, 29.7 × 21.2 cm, watermark similar to M.20
References: B.95; M.207 (before text, b); Sch.185 (before text, b)
Provenance: purchased from Colnaghi's, London, 1966
DÜRER 45 (P 2677 WHOLE SERIES)

Christ Taking Leave of his Mother, c.1508–9

(from *The Small Passion*, 8)
Woodcut, 12.5 × 97 cm; inscription in pencil 'Matth. İ5.25.', no watermark
References: B.21; M.132 (without text); Sch.193 (without text)
Provenance: purchased from Lyon & Turnbull, Edinburgh, 1967
DÜRER 2 (P 2693) · FIG.23

The Virgin Appearing to Saint John, 1511

(from *The Apocalypse*, title page; 2nd edition 1511, with Latin text on verso)
Woodcut, 39.3 × 28.1 cm, no watermark
References: B.60; M.163 (with text, b); Sch.111 (with text, b)
Provenance: purchased from Colnaghi's, London, 1964
DÜRER 46 (P 2665 WHOLE SERIES)

Christ Before Pilate, 1512

(from *The Engraved Passion*, 5)
Engraving, 11.7 × 7.5 cm, no watermark
Verso: inscription in brown ink 'R N [...]'
References: B.7; M.7 (b); Sch.49 (b)
Provenance: presented by the Royal Scottish Museum, Edinburgh, 1952
DÜRER 97 (P 2181)

Flagellation, 1512

(from *The Engraved Passion*, 6)
Engraving, 11.9 × 7.4 cm, no watermark
Verso: inscription in brown ink 'R N H [?]'
References: B.8; M.8 (c); Sch.50 (c)
Provenance: presented by the Royal Scottish Museum, Edinburgh, 1952
DÜRER 98 (P 2182)

Christ Crowned with Thorns, 1512

(from *The Engraved Passion*, 7)
Engraving, 11.7 × 7.4 cm, no watermark
Verso: inscription in brown ink 'R N [...]'
References: B.9; M.9 (a); Sch.51 (a)
Provenance: presented by the Royal Scottish Museum, Edinburgh, 1952
DÜRER 99 (P 2183)

Ecce Homo, 1512

(from *The Engraved Passion*, 8)
Engraving, 11.7 × 7.5 cm, no watermark
References: B.10; M.10 (b); Sch.52 (b)
Provenance: purchased (£38) by A. Maitland, 1916; Gift of Mr and Mrs Alexander Maitland, 1953
DÜRER 100 (P 2205)

Saint Jerome in a Cave, 1512

Woodcut, 17.4 × 13 cm, watermark similar to M.326 (c.1570?)
Verso: J. Reynold's stamp (Lugt 2364)
References: B.113; M.229; Sch.232. This is an impression of a hitherto unpublished second state.
Provenance: Sir Joshua Reynolds; otherwise unknown
DÜRER 6 · FIG.21

Knight, Death and Devil, 1513

Engraving, 24.4 × 18.9 cm, no watermark
References: B.98; M.74 (b/c); Sch.69 (b/c)
Provenance: purchased from C.G. Boerner, Düsseldorf, 1961
DÜRER 102 (P 2507)

Saint Jerome in his Study, 1514

Engraving, 27 × 20.6 cm, no watermark
References: B.60; M.59 (a); Sch.70 (a)
Provenance: purchased from C.G. Boerner, Düsseldorf, 1967
DÜRER 95 (P 2690) · FIG.1

Melencolia I (Melancholy), 1514

Engraving, 24.1 × 19 cm, watermark similar to M.46–8
Verso: inscription in pencil 'Melancholy 1514/ Albert Durer'; 'Mr Watson £1/15/-'
References: B.74; M.75 (2d/e); Sch.71 (2d/e)
Provenance: William Finlay Watson (Lugt 2599) [?]; presented by the Royal Scottish Museum, Edinburgh, 1952
DÜRER 96 (P 2170)

Landscape with the Cannon, 1518

Iron etching, 22.8 × 33.6 cm, watermark similar to M.116, unidentified countermark
Verso: inscriptions in black ink 'RSK'; 'No 118'
References: B.99; M.96 (with rust marks, b); Sch.85 (with rust marks, b)
Provenance: purchased from A.J. Mackenzie Stuart, Edinburgh, 1952
DÜRER 107 (P 2168) · FIG.2

Saint Anthony Reading, 1519

Engraving, 9.9 × 14.4 cm, no watermark
References: B.58; M.51 (a); Sch.87 (a)
Provenance: purchased from Colnaghi's, London, 1961
DÜRER 113 (P 2498) · FIG.15

Works by Other Artists

Anonymous artist, after Albrecht Dürer

The Circumcision, 1541(?)

(reduced copy in reverse after *The Life of the Virgin*, II, *c.*1504)
Engraving, 25.8 × 21.3 cm, trimmed(?), watermark similar to M.191 (Arnhem 1603), 346, 347 (both Arnhem 1614)
Signed and dated (?): 'O [or C] I 41' (in reverse)
Verso: inscription in pencil 'Compare/ with Chapmans/ W.F. Watson'
References: unpublished, the artist OI is probably not to be identified with G.K. Nagler, *Die Monogrammisten*, vol.4, Munich 1919, no.2639
Provenance: William Finlay Watson (Lugt 2599) [?]; transferred from the Scottish National Portrait Gallery, Edinburgh
DÜRER 168 · FIG.10

Anonymous German (Augsburg?) artist, in the style of Albrecht Dürer

*The Entombment of Christ, c.*1600

Engraving, 23.5 × 17.6 cm; falsely signed and dated 'AD' and '1507', no watermark
References: Nuremberg 1976, no. 113
Provenance: transferred from the Scottish National Portrait Gallery, Edinburgh
DÜRER 161 · FIG.17

Anonymous photographer

The Albrecht Dürer House in Nuremberg, *c.*1860s

Photograph (albumen print from collodion negative), 25.8 × 20.8 cm
References: unpublished
Provenance: album (PGP 237) possibly assembled by Walter Crum (1796–1867) and his family, Glasgow; purchased 1950
Scottish National Portrait Gallery, Edinburgh
PGP 237.12 · FIG.28

Nilz Böhme (born 1971)

Portrait of Pascal Hens, 2006

(poster advertising Kampa sporting goods)
Colour print, 83.9 × 59.3 cm
PRIVATE COLLECTION · FIG.32

Hendrick ter Brugghen (1588–1629), workshop of

The Beheading of Saint John the Baptist, *c.*1620–30

Oil on canvas, 167.6 × 217.8 cm
References: Leonard J. Slatkes and Wayne Franits, *The Paintings of Hendrick ter Brugghen 1588–1629*, Amsterdam 2007, no.R38
Provenance: presented to the Board of Manufactures for the future National Gallery of Scotland by James S. Wardrop, London, 1850
NG 28 · FIG.14

Hendrick Goltzius (1558–1617)

The Circumcision, 1594

Engraving, 49.1 × 36.4 cm
Verso: inscriptions in pencil 'Six./No 42' and 'Alb. Durer.'
References: Huigen Leeflang and Ger Luijten (eds), *Hendrick Goltzius (1558–1617): Drawings, Prints and Paintings*, exhibition catalogue, Amsterdam, New York and Toledo (OH) 2003, no.75.4
Provenance: unknown
DUTCH 215 · FIG.11

Hieronymus Greff (*c.*1460–after 1507), after Albrecht Dürer
The Beast with Two Horns Like a Lamb, 1502

(from *The Apocalypse*, II; copy after 1st edition 1498; with German text on verso)
Woodcut, 39 × 28 cm, no watermark
Verso: inscription in black ink 'Apocalypse of St. John/ Copied from Albert Durer same size as/ originals, "very finely executed" Bryan/ Jerome Greff native of Frankfort a pupil of Albert Durer/ published/ woodcuts in 1502'
References: Vogt 2008, no.I.13
Provenance: transferred from the Scottish National Portrait Gallery, Edinburgh
DÜRER 133 · FIG.5

Wenceslaus Hollar (1607–1677), after Albrecht Dürer
Portrait of Albrecht Dürer, 1645

(after a copy of Albrecht Dürer's painted *Self-portrait* of 1498, Museo del Prado, Madrid, inv. no.2179)
Etching, 21.8 × 15.9 cm, watermark similar to Heawood 2005 (Dartford 1656), cf. Heawood 1990 (Dutch 1652), unidentified countermark
References: Simon Turner, *Wenceslaus Hollar: Part III* (*The New Hollstein German Engravings, Etchings and Woodcuts 1400–1700*), Ouderkerk aan den Ijssel 2010, no.693
Provenance: William Findlay Watson Bequest, 1886
Scottish National Portrait Gallery, Edinburgh
FP I 48.3 · FIG.24

Hieronymus Hopfer (*c.*1500–1563?), after Albrecht Dürer
The Flight into Egypt, 1530s (?)

(reduced copy in reverse after *The Life of the Virgin*, 14, *c.*1504)
Iron etching, 22.4 × 15.6 cm, no watermark
Verso: inscription 'Flight into Egypt/Jerome Hopfer. /(Nuremberg circa 1535.)' and 'D. Hopfer'
References: Nuremberg 1978, no.109; Vogt 2008, no.167
Provenance: transferred from the Scottish National Portrait Gallery, Edinburgh
N101206SP1.1

Ottmar Hörl (born 1950), after Albrecht Dürer
Dürer Hare, 2003

(after the watercolour of 1502 in the Albertina, Vienna, inv.no.3073)
Multiple sculpture, painted plastic, 26 × 16 × 36 cm
PRIVATE COLLECTION

Marcantonio Raimondi (*c.*1480–before 1534), after Albrecht Dürer
*The Circumcision, c.*1506

(copy after *The Life of the Virgin*, II, *c.*1504)
Engraving, 29.1 × 21 cm; watermark similar to Heawood 1129, 1131–3 (Venice 1565–1610)
References: B.632; Nuremberg 1978, no.111
Provenance: transferred from the Scottish National Portrait Gallery, Edinburgh
DÜRER 9 · FIG.9

Marcantonio Raimondi (*c.*1480–before 1534), after Albrecht Dürer
*The Glorification of the Virgin, c.*1506

(copy after *The Life of the Virgin*, 20, *c.*1502)
Engraving, 29.8 × 21.6 cm, unidentified watermark (circle with letters PM [?])
References: B.637; Williamstown 1975, no.16
Provenance: purchased 2011
N1104200T.1 · FIG.6

Attributed to Jusepe de Ribera (1591–1652), after Albrecht Dürer
*Man Holding a Candlestick, c.*1620–30

(after *The Circumcision* from *The Life of the Virgin*, II, *c.*1504)
Pen and brush in black over black chalk, 42.5 × 28 cm; unidentified watermark (raising quadruped)
Reference: Keith Andrews, *Catalogue of German Drawings in the National Gallery of Scotland*, Edinburgh 1991, p.5, fig.16 (as [anonymous German] copy after Albrecht Dürer)
Provenance: David Laing Bequest to the Royal Scottish Academy, transferred 1910
D 1164 · FIG.12

John Runciman (1744–1768/69), after Albrecht Dürer

*Christ Taking Leave of his Mother, c.*1765
(after *The Small Passion*, 8, *c.*1508–9)
Oil on mahogany panel, 28.2 × 17.8 cm
References: David and Francina Irwin, *Scottish*

Painters: At Home and Abroad 1700–1900, London 1975, pp.111–12, pl.46
Provenance: Maurice Herbert Towneley, 3rd Lord O'Hagan; his sale London (Christie, Manson & Woods), 19 May 1939, lot 72 (£110/5/-); bought by Barbizon House (presumably Lockett Thomson), London; Walter Runciman, 2nd Baron and 1st Viscount Runciman of Doxford, to his death in 1949; his son Hon. Sir Steven Runciman to his death in 2000; Sir Steven Runciman Bequest, 2000
NG 2723 · FIG.22

Aegidius Sadeler (*c.*1570–1629), after Albrecht Dürer
*Virgin and Child in a Landscape, c.*1600

(after watercolour in the Albertina, Vienna, inv.no.3066)
Engraving, 32.1 × 24.3 cm (trimmed, without the inscription), no watermark
References: Nuremberg 1976, no.72
Provenance: unknown
DÜRER 130 (GERMAN 23)

William Bell Scott (1811–1890)
Albrecht Dürer in Nuremberg, 1854

Oil on canvas, 60.4 × 73 cm
References: Colin Thompson and Hugh Brigstocke, *National Gallery of Scotland: Shorter Catalogue*, Edinburgh 1978, p.98
Provenance: Mrs Ballantine, Edinburgh (1886); purchased from Aitken Dott & Son, Edinburgh, 1909
NG 969 · FIG.27

William Bell Scott (1811–1890)
Self-portrait, 1861

Watercolour over some pencil, 28 × 22.9 cm, signed and dated 'WBS [intertwined]/ Sepr 1861'
Reference: unpublished
Provenance: William Bell Scott; Alice Boyd; by descent; Penkill Castle sale, Girvan, Aryshire (Christie's Scotland Ltd), 15 December 1992, lot 145; purchased 1992
PG 2918
(FRAMED AS A DIPTYCH WITH PG 2919)

William Bell Scott (1811–1890)
Portrait of Alice Boyd, 1861

Watercolour over some pencil, 28 × 22.9 cm, signed and dated 'WBS [intertwined]/ Penkill/ July 1861'
Reference: unpublished
Provenance: William Bell Scott; Alice Boyd; by descent; Penkill Castle sale, Girvan, Aryshire (Christie's Scotland Ltd), 15 December 1992, lot 145; purchased 1992
PG 2919
(FRAMED AS A DIPTYCH WITH PG 2918)

William Bell Scott (1811–1890)
Albert Durer: His Life and Works. Including Autobiographical Papers and Complete Catalogues. With six etchings by the author, London 1869

PRIVATE COLLECTION

Wilhelm Seifert (1923–1984), after Albrecht Dürer
Praying Hands, 1957

(after the drawing of 1508 in the Albertina, Vienna, inv.no.3113)
Pencil, 28.6 × 22.5 cm
PRIVATE COLLECTION

Andries Jacobsz Stock (*c.*1580–after 1648), after Tommaso Vincidor (1493–1536)
Portrait of Albrecht Dürer, 1629

(after Vincidor's lost portrait painting of Albrecht Dürer of 1520)
Engraving, 22.2 × 16.7 cm, watermark similar to Churchill 56 (1768) and 69, unidentified countermark 'F RIEVE [...?] / FIN/AGENO [...]'
Verso: inscription 'Rare 31/6.'
References: Nuremberg 1976, no.97
Provenance: William Findlay Watson Bequest, 1886.
Scottish National Portrait Gallery, Edinburgh.
FP I 48.4 · FIG.25

Johannes Wierix (1549–*c.*1620), after Albrecht Dürer
Melencolia I (Melancholy), 1602

Engraving, 24.2 × 19 cm, no watermark
Verso: circular label in red 'Museum of Science & Art, Edinburgh/Industrial Art: 1894, No 148 (in black ink)'
References: Zsuzsanna van Ruyven-Zeman, *The Wierix Family: Part IX* (*Hollstein's Dutch & Flemish Etchings, Engravings and Woodcuts 1450–1700, vol.67*), Rotterdam 2004, no.2000
Provenance: presented by the Royal Scottish Museum, Edinburgh, 1952
DÜRER 128 (P 2171)
ILLUSTRATED ON PAGE 6

AUTHOR'S ACKNOWLEDGEMENTS

The idea for this display first emerged when Helen Smailes drew my attention to John Runciman's little panel *Christ Taking Leave of his Mother*, which is based on Dürer's print, and William Bell Scott's *Albrecht Dürer in Nuremberg*. I thank her for this initiation and her support throughout the project. I am grateful for advice, encouragement, and support generously received from Janis Adams, Christopher Baker, Giulia Bartrum, Peter Black, Nilz Böhme, Hannah Brocklehurst, Michael Clarke, Shona Corner, Yasmin Doosry, Kerry Eldon, Thomas Eser, Robert Ferguson, Duncan Forbes, Amy Golahny, Sina Haug, Reiner Haussherr, Lars Hendrikman, Pascal Hens, Ottmar Hörl und Cornelia Regner-Hörl, Valerie Hunter, Sarah Jeffcott, Nicola Kalinsky, Barbara Kaulbach, Gudrun Knaus, Paul Knolle, Samantha Lagneau, Kristin Lohse Belkin, Elinor McMonagle, Charlotte Park, Roderick Pelser, Jacqueline Ridge, Louise Rowlands, Rainer Schoch, Klaus Schreiner and Birgit Geißler, Olivia Sheppard, Janice Slater, Leigh Stevenson, Ulrike Swoboda, Christine Thompson, Jaap van der Veen, Robert Wenley, Aidan Weston-Lewis, and the National Galleries of Scotland's art handling team. I am particularly grateful to Graeme Gollan who conserved and examined the works on paper for this display, reviewed and x-rayed watermarks, helped with the checklist and found time for enjoyable and fruitful discussions with me. Many thanks go to Michael Bury, Thomas Schauerte and Jeffrey Chipps Smith who kindly read the draft text and offered valuable comments. The German Consulate General Edinburgh supported research towards this booklet and I wish to particularly thank Consul General Wolfgang Mössinger and Consul Beate Bidenbach. This publication would not have seen the light of day without the enthusiastic and generous support of Martin Adam and William Zachs, for which I am most grateful.

I dedicate this little book to the memory of my father who first nourished the love for art in me.

CTS